STRATEGIC
WARFARE
IN
BED

REHOBOTH
BIBLE MINISTRIES
PUBLICATIONS

EstheticCommunications

STRATEGIC WARFARE IN BED

IN

BED

TAIWO OLUSEGUN AYENI

authorHOUSE®

AuthorHouse™
1663 Liberty Drive
Bloomington, IN 47403
www.authorhouse.com
Phone: 1 (800) 839-8640

KJV
Scripture quotations marked KJV are from the Holy Bible, King James Version (Authorized Version). First published in 1611. Quoted from the KJV Classic Reference Bible, Copyright © 1983 by The Zondervan Corporation.

AMP
Scripture quotations marked AMP are from The Amplified Bible, Old Testament copyright © 1965, 1987 by the Zondervan Corporation. The Amplified Bible, New Testament copyright © 1954, 1958, 1987 by The Lockman Foundation. Used by permission. All rights reserved.

GNT
Scripture quotations marked GNT are taken from the Good News Translation — Second Edition. Copyright © 1992 by American Bible Society. Used by permission. All rights reserved.

Published by AuthorHouse 08/14/2015

ISBN: 978-1-5049-2938-7 (sc)
ISBN: 978-1-5049-2937-0 (e)

Print information available on the last page.

Rehoboth Bible Ministries Inc Publications
2304 Oak Lane, 3A Suite 7,
Grand Prairie, Texas, 75051, USA
Tel: (972) 345-5357, (972) 742-7365
E-mail: taayeni@rehobothbministries.org
Website: www.rehobothbministries.org

Edited and Desktop Published by:
Rehoboth Consultancy Service
2304 Oak Ln, 3A Ste #7,
Grand Prairie, Texas, 75051, USA
Tel: 972-742-7365,
www.rehobothbministries.org

Cover Design by
Esthetic Communications
1102 W. Pioneer Pkwy, Suite #115
Grand Prairie, Texas, 75051, USA
Office (972) 602-2475; Cell (817) 659-5576

Dedication

I dedicate this book to the Almighty God who stirred my heart in this direction. May His name be praised.

Acknowledgments

I wish to acknowledge the support of my beloved wife Dr. (Mrs.) Abidemi Olubisi Ayeni, who sacrificially offers herself in order to see me succeed in ministry. To Rere, my son and Ore, my daughter who with my wife, have listened to me share these thoughts before going public, God bless you all.

I sincerely appreciate and acknowledge Rev. (Dr.) Moses Aransiola, whose mentoring role and materials provided me with the resource for this work. Thank you sir.

I also appreciate the pastors of my home Church, Household of Faith, Arlington, Pastor Ebenezer Ropo and Pastor (Mrs.) Laide Ropo-Tusin, who provided me the platform to first teach this message at the 911 Conference, 2012.

My thanks also go to my Church family members who, in spite of my absence from their midst, always gladly welcome me back, and patiently listened when I am invited to preach.

To my Prayer School Team, we shall all grow in grace together. You're all blessed.

To my beloved Pastor Abiodun Coker, and Pastor Femi Agiri, my friends and prayer partners who the Lord used to rigorously edit this work. God bless you richly sirs.

And to all the churches of God, their pastors and brethren where I had preached these messages in various forms, you are all appreciated. Keep pressing on, you shall see the tops of the mountains in Jesus name. Remain blessed and highly favored.

Taiwo Olusegun Ayeni
March, 2013

Table of Contents

Preface

Why is your bed strategic? It is because the place where you sleep is a site of divine renewal or satanic regression. You could be either made or marred on your bed. Lying on your bed in the solemnity of the day or serenity of the night, you can initiate, maintain, and sustain fruitful thinking that will change your life. Great thoughts of glorious happenings could be inspired on your bed as you thoughtfully guard your hearts in deep search for divine mysteries:

There is a spirit in man, the inspiration of the Lord giveth them understanding. - Job 32:8

Such deep reflections of the night have made great men out of many, who hitherto were not born with great advantages. So many people, believers inclusive, allow their minds to wander away in the thoughts of the night, not knowing that the outcome of the events of the following day is being established during this time.

Some lie dejectedly on their beds, devastated because of the disappointments or failures encountered during the day. They lose their peace and find no rest but instead an anxiety-infused night. A bad night will produce a grumpy and agitated morning, and the cycle continues.

God ordained your bed principally as a place of rest, renewal and refreshing. As you sleep and wake up, you are empowered or energized to wake up to another enterprising day of fulfilling God's purpose for you on earth. When you miss this opportunity, what God ordained for you may never be realized until your habits change.

It is equally true that prolonged lack of rest or sleep results in stress-induced insanity, and sleep is a potent medicine for good health. Everyone should be wise enough to prepare for the night, just as they do for the morning. A man must prepare for his day and night in order to make it in life, because the wicked one is waiting in the wings to sow evil seed in the lives of men.

Those who know the importance of the bed have been inspired with deep revelation, instruction, invention, creative direction, and also enjoyed needed solutions to prolonged problems. Many who understand the importance of the bed as a place of power do not go to bed carelessly. They have come to know the bed is a place of night-gate warfare.

All kinds of battle wait for the night when the souls of men are weary from the day's labor. Many such attacks are launched and fought upon our beds. Several beloved souls have gone through inexplicable nightmares, late night trauma, and barrages of harrowing thoughts that make even bold men tremble. It happens because our minds are viable grounds for the devil to display his morbid wares, while we engage in *"...disquieting thoughts from the visions of the night, When deep sleep falls on men."* - Job 4:13

Resist the plan of the devil to engage your minds negatively, and strategically win the battle over your mind upon your bed. It is well, see you at His throne room in Jesus name!

Taiwo Olusegun Ayeni
January, 2013

1

CHAPTER

A New Altar

"Then Elijah said to all the people, "Come near to me." So all the people came near to him. And he repaired the altar of the Lord which had been torn down."

- (I kings 18:30)

Anyone who intends to finish strong must endeavor to have a vibrant prayer altar. Every altar built is inspired by covenant encounter with God e.g. Abraham, Isaac and Jacob raised between them seven (7) altars. No man builds an altar without first having a divine encounter with God, and also no altar is raised without a covenant backing it. The strength of any altar is determined by the power of the covenant backing it.

For example, the blood of Jesus, is the token backing our altar of relationship with Him. That's why we have the audacity to plead His blood when our position is threatened! The powers backing formidable altars are potent, hence the reason Balaam raised seven (7) altars in order to release a curse on Israel. Why seven (7) altars? It was to match and neutralize the potency of the seven (7) Patriarchal altars raised by Abraham, Isaac and Jacob. But when his attempts failed, he advised Balak to invite them to the activities of Moab where they fell, through whoredom and idolatry. For this *"...the anger of the LORD was kindled against Israel."* (Numbers 25:1-3).

A) What Is An Altar?

An altar is a place of meeting with God. When your altar of prayer is pure and therefore formidable, God responds to it with fresh fire. Therefore, the key to bringing down fresh fire is to repair your broken down altar. Without a righteous or formidable altar, there can be no fresh fire. Every good altar carries a sacrifice on it, hence the Psalmist says:

"Gather my saints together unto me; those that have made a covenant with me by sacrifice." (Psalm 50:5)

Gather them based on covenant of life and peace (Malachi 2:4-5). This sacrificial covenant offered on pure altar of the heart carries divine benefits (Isaiah 54:10).

Just as the physical altar is expected to be pure, your heart also must be pure (Psalm 51:17; 34:18). This is the reason you must guide your heart with all diligence (Proverbs 4:23).

The state of your heart will affect the answer to your prayer, if not guarded. Specifically, impure hearts hinder divine visitation. God keeps His promise to be present where two or three are gathered (Mathew 18:20), and when He comes, He looks for who to bless with deliverance, but the state of our hearts sometimes hinders. The scriptures below reveal what He would have done if our hearts were right:

"For, behold, the LORD will come with fire, and with his chariots like a whirlwind, to render his anger with fury, and his rebuke with flames of fire. For by fire and by his sword will the LORD plead with all flesh: and the slain of the LORD shall be many."- Isaiah 66:15-16

"Out of Zion, the perfection of beauty, God hath shined. Our God shall come, and shall not keep silence: a fire shall devour before him, and it shall be very tempestuous round about him." - Psalm 50:2-3

When you harbor grudges, covetousness, bitterness, malice, evil competition, un-forgiveness, contention, and lust then you cannot experience fresh fire. Many prayers offered do not get to the ears of God, because they are from impure hearts or altars. Your heart is the first house of prayer, and if it is impure, your prayer to God is zero. As a result, there would be no testimonies recorded on your altar of prayer.

An impure heart introduces corruption into your prayers. God will not answer the prayer of active, deliberate or intentional sinners until they repent! (Proverbs 15:8, 28:9; John. 9:31) Sinful hearts inevitably result in wasted effort in prayer (Isaiah 26:15-18). This is the picture of many of us today.

The summary of Isaiah 26:16-18 is itemized below:

- we are pregnant with ideas or burdens but brought forth wind.
- no deliverance wrought in our land.
- neither have we won souls for Christ as expected.
- Yet we have **"...poured out..."** our hearts in prayer when thy chastening was upon us (Isaiah 26:16 KJV).

The secret of those who make impact in prayer is that they seek God with pure hearts. Before praying they:

- consecrate their hearts
- invite the cross to deal with their hearts
- make sure that self is on the cross, and Christ is on the throne of their lives.
- sanctify the altars of their hearts before placing the sacrifices on them.

Consequently, when these are done fire always fall from heaven. Fire would never fall upon a desecrated altar! That's why my mentor, a notable vessel in the area of prayer said, I quote:

"The heart of the matter in prayer, is the matter of the heart." - Rev. (Dr.) Moses Aransiola.

While the Psalmist on the one hand also points at this fact: ***"...a broken and a contrite heart, O God, thou wilt not despise."*** (Psalm 51:17); the Lord also reaffirms it in Mathew 5:8:

"Blessed are the pure in heart, for they shall see God."

In spite of this obvious warnings, impure thoughts have distanced many of us from God's presence.

Furthermore, the Psalmist, in Psalm 24:3-4, raises the question about who is qualified to ascend the hill of God? He confirms that they are those with clean hands, pure hearts and souls not lifted up to vanity. Not only must these people be qualified to ascend, they must also be spiritually fit to stand, abide and dwell. They must speak ***"...the truth from (their) hearts."*** (Psalm 15:2).

Speaking the truth from the heart is one of the conditions required to abide and dwell in God's holy presence. We read again in Psalm 24:6 how the Lord viewed this category of believers - they ***"...are the generation of them that seek thy face, O Lord."*** Or those whom He allows to see His face.

To prevail then in prayer, necessity is laid upon us to cultivate purity of heart, and seek to be intentionally pure. When you do so, your blessings are already waiting for you. It's important because out of your heart flows the issues of life (Proverbs 4:23). And it is what comes out of you that defiles you (Mark 7:20-23). Be not deceived if you want to receive answer to prayer - check your heart condition!

Know that a man with a defiled heart is like an idolater who worships the object of his defilement; while a woman with a defiled heart is like a harlot running after other gods (men) - because her survival depends on them. For your reckoning, idolatry and immorality are two vices that God passionately hates, and for these His anger was kindled and He brought judgment on the children of Israel (Numbers 25:3, 4-9).

The subtlety of idolatry is so disarming that many unknowingly fall for its compelling allurement. Balaam had deep insight about this reality. Hence, what he could not achieve through cursing Israel, he succeeded in doing by advising Balak to invite them unto the sacrifices of their gods. And when he did, and Israel responded, they were influenced to commit idolatry and adultery with the Midianites!

"And Israel joined himself unto Baalpeor..." (Numbers 25:1-3).

B) What Is Idolatry?

Before I define idolatry, I wish to quote from the book **"Keep Yourself From Idols"** written by David Alsobrook. In defining idolatry, he broke it into two words that we could conveniently relate with, and brought out the reality of this practice by showing the active and passive participants of idol worship. As I quote, the author began with the question:

"Idolizer or Idolater?

In classical Greek literature this word is used for a literal statue or even for a concept of the mind. In this regard I believe that many of God's people have a particular concept, teaching, or pet doctrine which they will not submit to God's correction as it relates to the pet doctrine's imbalance or error. These "sacred cows" thus qualify as idols in the Greek meaning of the word. An "idolizer" is someone who has a particular idol, but whose life is not wholly given to idols. Such a person whose life is full of idols is properly called an "idolater" and has no inheritance in the kingdom of God." (pg 55 - 56)

Furthermore, the idolizer makes a god out of things he or she passionately cares about e.g. cars, designer wears, electronic gadgets, furniture items, doting on child, wife or husband etc. He or she does everything to preserve the "sanctity" of these "perishable items" and carelessly allow them to replace God in his or her willing hearts.

While the idolizer is a passive worshipper; the idolater is a very active one, and his or her life revolves round the object of worship. The object of worship dictates his or her life. He or she actively lives and walks in the tenacity of the worship of idols in obvious rebellion to God's commands. Without any contradiction, God hates idolatry with great passion, and does not mince words in condemning it in every way possible:

"Confounded be all they ...that boast themselves in idols..." (Psalm 97:7).

Furthermore, the Holy Spirit through John the Beloved succinctly warns us in I John 5:21: *"...Keep yourself from idols..."*

God seeks to reward our righteous lives, but many of us who have idols in our hearts have denied Him the opportunity to bless us. If we will take the path King David took in addressing these issues, our battles are more than won. We are taught in Psalm 18:20-21, that God rewards our righteousness:

"The LORD rewarded me according to my righteousness; according to the cleanness of my hands hath he recompensed me. For I have kept the ways of the LORD, and have not wickedly departed from my God."

Walking in righteousness is not just a must, it should be a matter of life and death to us. We must choose to do the right things whatever happens, let it count. The Daily Devotion of January 4th, 2013, precisely presents this thought thus:

"Salvation is not just the position of righteousness you hold before God, but a condition of righteousness you live out before others every day."

For, example, David did not depend on grace and mercy alone by assumption, he acted on God's word by forsaking impure thoughts that translate in impure works! He joyfully and victoriously declares: ***"I have kept the ways of the LORD, and have not wickedly departed from my God."*** (Psalm 18:21). Amen to that. Thereafter, his righteousness counted for him in the time of desperate need.

While I agree that we are bombarded daily by the avalanche of impure sights on our streets, offices, neighborhood, and sometimes our churches; and the fact that the television, and internet are the worst culprits, bringing evil images right into the confines of our homes, we must do everything to resist, and we have no excuse when we fall!

We have enough examples and warnings from men who have faced similar challenges and have survived it. For example in the book of Lamentations 3:51 we read the very profound lamentation of a man viciously assaulted by the barrage of evil in his city:

"Mine eye affected mine heart because of all the daughters of my city."

The lesson here is, what we feed our eyes will touch our hearts, and affect us emotionally, especially if it is immoral. But Brother Job precisely instructs us on how to deal with this evil weapon of mass destruction, which Satan has successfully wielded against believers, and have caused the fall of many. Job's solution is: ***"I have made a covenant with mine eyes; Why then should I look upon a young woman?"*** (Job 31:1)

Proverbs 4:23, 25-27 cemented the counsel by encouraging us to guard our hearts with all diligence, ponder the paths of our feet, and let our eyes not wander away, but look straight before us. Like the decision Job personally made, the solution against beholding evil is to covenant your eyes from seeing it. If we are going to be revived and finish strong, we must treat the issue of the purity of our hearts seriously. Only pure vessels pray pure prayers therefore *"...flee youthful lust..."*

C) The Two Altars

The prayer that produces results is not only based on vibrant altar, but also on the covenant POWER backing it (Psalm 63:1-3)! To generate that power two specific altars must be diligently serviced and these are the altars of:

1) Incense (Prayer - Revelation 8:3-4; Psalm 141:2)
2. Sacrifice (Praise - Hebrews 13:15; Psalm 34:1)

To generate POWER, Prayer and Praise altars are covenant altars on which we must offer unto God incense and sacrifice always (Psalm 65:1-2). Even though they are types of prayer on their own, yet they complement each other. While one is expressed in spoken words, the other is expressed in songs or poems. We also have included in the praise category Thanksgiving and Worship as other forms of prayer.

1). Altar of Incense (Prayer)

No man gets anything done with or for God without prayer, and God operates on the principle of asking and receiving (Matthew 7:7). Because He is a just God, who gives everyone equal opportunity, He awaits your cry in prayer. The person who does not pray is only hurting himself. God does nothing but in answer to prayer. He is a patient God and is always willing to wait patiently for you to call. Knowing the critical nature and significance of prayer, King David vowed to pray daily unto God:

"My voice shalt thou hear in the morning, O Lord; in the morning will I direct my prayer unto thee, and will look up." - Psalm 5:3

As he cultivated a daily prayer relationship with God, and enjoyed its indescribable benefits, he had a rethink on praying once a day. He resolved to move from once a day to thrice - morning, noon, and evening - (Psalm 55:17). By this he figured out he would enjoy deeper fellowship with God as he related with Him.

Within a short period, he equally realized spending three times a day with God in prayer was insufficient. He recalled His loving-kindness, protection and righteous judgments and therefore opted to do it seven times a day! His reason for praying seven times a day is also mentioned in the passage:

"Seven times a day do I praise thee because of thy righteous judgments." Psalm 119:164

Being so much appreciative of God, and always looking out for ways to express it, he again thoughtfully arrived at a point in his life to notice that even seven times a day was not enough to praise God. Having considered His faithfulness, and his mighty deliverance from the hands of King Saul multiple times, he decided to praise God at all times meeting the Holy Spirit counsel of praying without ceasing (I Thess. 5:17). The Psalmist declares, quoting him:

"I will bless the Lord at all times: his praise shall continually be in my mouth." - Psalm 34:1

This decision also meets the Holy Spirit's expectation in Hebrews 13:15 for every believer to continually offer sacrifice of praise to God as we worship Him:

"By him therefore let us offer the sacrifice of praise to God continually, that is, the fruit of our lips giving thanks to his name."

Benefits of A Vibrant Altar of Prayer

When a formidable altar of prayer is raised several things happen, and these are itemized below:

a) Fire falls - Elijah in I Kings 18:30 repaired the broken down altar before he called upon the name of the Lord who answered by fire (I kings 18:36-38). His effort revealed to us the ingredients required to activate a vibrant altar. Sequentially, he raised an altar in the name of the Lord (sure foundation), provided the wood or fuel, and placed the sacrifice on the altar. He poured water (the undiluted word of God) upon the sacrifice, and then called upon the name of the Lord.

Many of us symbolically need to pour buckets of water upon our sacrifices, that we may be spiritually washed by the washing of the water of His word (Eph. 5:26). The water of the word is capable of removing spots and impurities, if any, in our lives. This is necessary if our sacrifices are to be acceptable in His sight. Logically though, it is not water you need when you want your altar to catch fire, you need gas oil or petrol, but God's ways are past finding out.

We also observe that Elijah was strategic in his approach and timing. He waited till the time of the offering of the evening sacrifice to call on the name of the Lord and then fire fell (v36-38). This signifies the importance of night/bedtime prayer, and the fact that fire purifies everything on our altar.

b) The heathen gets convicted and converted: In verse 39, immediately the heathen saw the fire fall, they reacted positively by falling on their faces in worship, and began to proclaim the greatness of God, as distinct from Baal a small god.

"And when all the people saw it, they fell on their faces: and they said, The Lord, he is God; the Lord, he is the God."

When people see signs they believe, and God has called us to be proof producers. If your Christianity is not evidenced based, you are robbing the kingdom of necessary souls that ought to have been won by the signs and wonders God planned to do through you. This cannot be done except you have a vibrant altar of prayer.

c) **The enemy falls under judgment.** Immediately the fire fell, and the people gave glory to God, Elijah, commanded that the prophets of Baal should be arrested.

"...And they took them: and Elijah brought them down to the brook Kishon, and slew them there." (v40)

The enemies become easy preys when you are empowered from your altar of prayer. The reason they boast now about their prowess against you, is because they have not witnessed the signs, and wonders you are supposed to be. Arise, repair your altar, take the battle to the gates of the enemy, and be the sign and wonders you ought to be!

d) **It inspires divine revelation** - a pure and effective altar inspires divine revelation from the presence of the Lord. Elijah with audacity told Ahab to get up and eat *"...for there is a sound of abundance of rain."* (v41). The nation had been waiting for rain, until the man with a formidable altar showed up with a word from God.

e) **It emboldens the beneficiary of the empowered altar, who is inspired to engage in divine PUSH "Pray Until Something Happens"** (v42). The interesting account here is while Elijah went up to pray until something happened, Ahab went up to eat. It is a choice we make whether to pray, or be a prey.

Elijah made the right choice *"...casting himself down upon the earth, and put his face between his knees"* and offered a desperate cry unto God. When in a few moments later he connected with God, he received the miracle answer, and told his servant to go *"...look toward the sea..."* (v43) But he came back declaring he saw nothing, and the man of God sent him back several times, because he had been assured by God that rain was about to fall. Wait until you see your change come (Job 14:14).

f) A formidable altar inspires faith that does not give up. When Elijah's servant returned with no good news, he sent him back seven times until he got the answer *"Go again seven times."* (v43). This is a clear picture of praying without ceasing, and never giving up until you touch the answer to prayer. Many give up easily because they lack the faith to continue. You must believe that He is, and He is a re-warder of those who diligently seek Him (Hebrews 11:6).

g) Praying till you get result is a product of resilience in prayer. Resilience or consistent focus in prayer inspires answer to your request. You must be determined to acquire the fire to meet your desire. Elijah did and his servant returned with the desired report *"...Behold there ariseth a little cloud out of the sea, like a man's hand..."* (v44).

h) Formidable altar guarantees rain. The heaven that was black with clouds and heavy with rain, had no choice but to release its contents in massive torrents of rain (v45). But before it fell, Elijah prepared Ahab to take off in his chariot, so that the rain would not stop him. The man who went to eat when others prayed, will not outrun the one who did, to the gates of blessings. God's hand fell on Elijah, and gave him grace to outrun King Ahab's in his chariot to the gates of Jezreel.

2. Altar of Sacrifice (Praise)

Praise is not just only prayer, it is also an instrument in prayer,- the power that oils the engine of prayer or better put, complements prayer. For this reason, it is a necessary requirement for answer to prayer. God cannot resist the praise of an upright man, and in fact He inhabits our praise (Psalm 22:3). Not only that, He credits the one who praise, and shows him or her His salvation (Psalm 50:23). We see God's mind earlier in the same passage:

"Offer unto God thanksgiving; and pay thy vows unto the most High: And call upon me in the day of trouble: I will deliver thee, and thou shalt glorify me." (v14-15)

Note the last phrase *"...and thou shalt glorify me."* How do we glorify Him? We glorify him by offering Him praise. This is confirmed in v23 of the same chapter in reference: *"Whoso offereth praise glorifieth me:..."*

The Power of Praise

Just as when incense (prayer) is offered something happens; also when sacrifice (praise) is offered some - thing happens. What happens? Let us eamine them below:

a) It makes the heavens to declare the righteous Acts of God - our examples here are Paul and Silas, who offered praise to God at midnight, and God showed up via an earthquake, and *"...the foundations of the prison were shaken and immediately all the doors were opened, and every one's bands were loosed."* - Acts 16:25-26

Two things obvious here are first, all the doors of opportunities that were shut against them were forced open. And second, every evidence of satanic bondage that kept them bound was loosed without any resistance from hell. Praise inspires divine freedom from the captives of the mighty, and the prey of the terrible ones, whether they like it or not (Isaiah 49:24-26).

b) It glorifies God - the keeper of the prison witnessed the visitation of God to Paul and Silas. He saw the glory of God and trembled!

"And the keeper of the prison awaking out of his sleep, and seeing the prison doors open, he drew out his sword, and would have killed himself, supposing that the prisoners had been fled. But Paul cried with a loud voice, saying, Do thyself no harm: for we

are all here. Then he called for a light, and sprang in, and came trembling..." (v27-30)

c) It makes God to reveal his salvation - the keeper of the prison after having witnessed God's visitation, *"...fell down before Paul and Silas, And brought them out, and said, Sirs, what must I do to be saved?"* (v30). There is nowhere in this passage where it is revealed that either Paul or Silas preached to him before he came to ask them how he could be saved. The miracle he experienced was enough message to convince him of God's saving grace. When we offer praise, God will show us His salvation (Psalm 50:23).

d) It reveals God as the Jehovah the man of war - when we praise God, He shows up in our battles and takes it up for us. He fights our battles as we sit at his right hand till He makes our enemies our footstool (Ps 110:1). He fought for Israel in 2 Chronicles 20:22:

"And when they began to sing and to praise, the LORD set ambushments against the children of Ammon, Moab, and mount Seir, which were come against Judah; and they were smitten."

e) It opens a door for divine provision and victory - when Elisha needed a word for the kings in battle, he asked for a minstrel and as he began to play the word of God in provision and victory came as we read in the of 2 Kings 3:15-18 below:

"And he said, Thus saith the LORD, Make this valley full of ditches. For thus saith the LORD, Ye shall not see wind, neither shall ye see rain; yet that valley shall be filled with water, that ye may drink, both ye, and your cattle, and your beasts. And this is but a light thing in the sight of the LORD: he will deliver the Moabites also into your hand."

f) It brings about deliverance from evil spirits - when Saul was under the torment of evil spirits, his officials advised him to look for someone who could play the harp so that he might find relief from his torment. Saul therefore asked them to look for such a man, and he was informed about David. Saul immediately sent to Jesse: *"... saying, Let David, I pray thee, stand before me; for* *he hath found favour in my sight. And it came to pass, when the evil spirit from God was upon Saul, that David took an harp, and played with his hand: so Saul was refreshed, and was well, and the evil spirit departed from him."* - I Samuel 16:22-23

Praise, Thanksgiving, Worship and Prayer Complement each other.

As mentioned earlier, we can conclude then that praise, thanksgiving, worship and prayer all work together. They are none exclusive; so do not hold on to the statement **"If prayer does not work try praise."**

It is a misconception, because praise, thanksgiving and worship are in themselves prayers. Jesus gave thanks at the tomb of Lazarus and received quick answer to His prayer (John 11:40-42) Therefore, offer praise to glorify him. If you order your conversation or life aright God will reveal to you the secret of his deliverance (Praise - Psalm 59:16-17 and Prayer - Isaiah 40:29-31).

2

CHAPTER

Sing Aloud Upon Your Beds

"Let the saints be joyful in glory: let them sing aloud upon their beds." - Psalm 149:5

The desire of God for us is to be active praise worshippers, and this is expressed almost everywhere in the Bible. We are called to be true worshippers, who praise Him in spirit and in truth. And as we remain in His presence, we will experience the fullness of joy and pleasures for evermore (Psalm 16:11). But due to our lack of understanding of the potency of praise, we restrict it only to either Church meeting, or during our time of personal devotion. God would rather want us to praise Him at all times and even on our beds!

God's desire for how our night should end is clearly expressed in Psalm 149:5 which I will encourage you to pay close attention to. His desire is for you to be joyful in the glory of the miracles He is working in your life. Never allow a day to end without having one thing or the other to thank Him for - even as you lie on your bed. Your bed is a strategic place of warfare. This is one reason why the Holy Spirit puts these verses of scriptures in the context of warfare. You may wonder what has singing aloud upon your beds got to do with warfare? It has a lot.

First of all, if you recall the outcome of Paul and Silas' praising God at midnight, it would give you a better understanding of the potency of praise. Secondly, if you reflect on the fact that whatever engages your mind on your bed will have control of you in the night season. Your bed is a place where powerful thought processes are initiated. Many are either made or marred on their beds!

While our bed is supposed to be a place of rest, renewal, refreshing and restoration, for many it has become a place of eating: ***"...the bread of sorrows,"*** (Psalm 127:2). Evil thoughts of failure, defeat, disappointment, discouragement, and deaths through suicide are orchestrated in the site of rest. Many who also give up on life do so most of the time upon their beds! And those who succeeded by grace, from this destructive affliction, rose up from their beds to confront and resist the devil. They refused to throw in the towel, and encouraged themselves in the Lord as they fought (I Samuel 30:6).

Furthermore, it is sad to observe that several innocent, but ignorant souls have been spiritually attacked, and bound on their beds. While many take for granted what happens while sleeping either during the day or at night, evil seeds of failure, poverty, sickness and death are sowed into people's lives as they sleep carelessly (Mathew 13:25).

Why is your bed strategic? Because the place where you sleep is a site of divine renewal or satanic regression. You could either be made or marred on your bed. Lying on your bed in the solemnity of day or serenity of night, you can initiate, maintain, and sustain fruitful thinking that will change your life. Great thoughts of glorious happenings could be inspired on your bed as you thoughtfully guard your hearts in deep search for divine mysteries:

"There is a spirit in man, the inspiration of the Lord giveth them understanding." - Job 32:8

Such deep reflections of the night have made great men of many, who were not born with great advantages. So many people, believers inclusive, allow their minds to wander away in the thoughts of the night, not knowing that the outcome of the events of the following day is established during this time.

Some lie dejectedly on their beds, devastated because of the disappointments or failures encountered during the day. They lose their peace and find no rest, but instead have an anxiety-infused night. A bad night will produce a grumpy and agitated morning, and the cycle continues.

Sleeping when it is required is great. This is because so many of us damage our health through indiscrete endless vigils that wear us out bodily without making room for sleep or rest. We carry on as if it does not matter. Yet prolonged lack of rest or sleep results in stress-induced insanity, and sleep is a potent medicine for good health. In a nutshell, it is good to praise God and sleep - find a balance as you do both. Everyone should be wise enough to prepare for the night, just as the morning. A man must prepare for his day and night in order to make it in life, because the wicked one is waiting in the wings to sow evil seed.

Those who know the importance of the bed have been inspired with deep revelation, instruction, invention, creative direction, and also enjoyed needed solutions to prolonged problems. Also those who know the bed as a place of power do not go to bed carelessly, they are aware it is a place of night-gate warfare. All kinds of battle wait for the night when the souls of men are weary from the day's labor. Many such attacks are launched and fought upon our beds. Several beloved souls have gone through inexplicable nightmares, late night trauma, and barrages of harrowing thoughts that make even bold men tremble. It happens because our minds are viable grounds for the devil to display his morbid wares, while we engage in: *...disquieting thoughts from the visions of the night, When deep sleep falls on men."* - Job 4:13

When deep sleep ought to provide you with divine rest, what are you engaged in? Depressive, careless thoughts of despair and hopelessness as if there is no God? The doorway to satanic oppression is a mind open to anger or bitterness inspired by the depressing thoughts of the night, that weigh men down, and produce nothing but fruits of fear, helplessness, and hopelessness. Whatever you allow will take control of you, that is why the Bible commands you to submit to God and then resist the devil (James 4:7).

King David knew this so much that he expressed the blessings that follow the divine adherence to the proper use of the bed in Psalms 63:5-6.

"My soul shall be satisfied as with marrow and fatness; and my mouth shall praise thee with joyful lips: When I remember thee upon my bed, and meditate on thee in the night watches."

May I quickly say here that such prayer and meditation on your bed must be a matter of the heart. The prayer without the heart is rebellion against God, and it is empty noise that will receive no reward. Many have spent precious time howling upon their beds for nothing and God was not in the midst of their cry! It was not a cry from the heart but a make-believe charade.

"Woe unto them! for they have fled from me... And they have not cried unto me with their heart, when they howled upon their beds:..." - Hosea 7:13-14 (KJV)

Let your prayer not just be a mental or mechanical response to God. Do it with the whole of your heart knowing that God responds to a broken and a contrite heart (Psalm 51:17). Let your heart be the garden in which the seeds of prayer and praise are sown, and wait patiently for the fruits to begin to manifest. It surely will.

The sad thing obvious in this matter, is that some do not see the role they play in inviting the nightmares they suffer. They inadvertently created a doorway for their affliction through anger or bitterness. It is true that whatever wound you nurture will fester. In spite of this, some like Job have erroneously accused God of causing their problems.

"When I say, 'My bed will comfort me, My couch will ease my complaint,' Then you scare me with dreams And terrify me with visions,..." - Job 7:13-14

The question is:

"Why complain in the first place? Why not turn your complaint to prayer? Why take it so much to heart in anger or bitterness that it attracts satanic retributions?"

Beware, your thoughts on your bed is crucial, and has spiritual implications. Manage your thoughts well, so that you do not become a prey.

While the bed is a potent site of inspiration and turn around in life, the wicked use their beds to device diabolical and deeply thought-through evils beyond human comprehension. They thereafter go ahead to execute it because it is in their power to do so (Psalm 36:4).

"He deviseth mischief upon his bed; he setteth himself in a way that is not good; he abhorreth not evil."

Also in Micah 2:1 we read the following scary words:

"WOE TO those who devise iniquity and work out evil upon their beds! When the morning is light, they perform and practice it because it is in their power." (AMP)

What do they do specifically?

"They covet fields and seize them, and houses and take them away; they oppress and crush a man and his house, a man and his inheritance." (v2 AMP)

They thought these evils through upon their beds! This is an abuse of God's formidable weapon of transformative change, rest and pre-emptive and protective warfare. God would not spare people like these hence He declares in v3:

"...Behold against this family I am planning a disaster from which you cannot remove your necks, nor will you be able to walk erect; for it will be an evil time."

Such is the anger of God against the deliberate abuse emanating from the bed. Whichever way you want to view it, the bed is defiled daily not through immorality alone, but either as a springboard for thinking up evils against innocent victims, or a battleground for terminating visions, and destinies of vulnerable souls.

Those who give up on life start the journey to depressive destruction when lying upon their beds. They become vulnerable one step at a time without their thoughts being arrested or replaced with the right one, till it gets out of hand. The devil is very strategic, hence he waits patiently to do battle with your mind, at the time when you are most vulnerable. That is at the time, when on your bed, the full weight and the realization of the day's challenges are fully offloaded on your minds.

The challenges of the day are usually kept in abeyance by the day's activities until you hit your bed at night. Then the floodgates of evil thoughts begin, with the worst negative outcomes you could have ever imagined. This **"False Evidence Appearing Real"** (FEAR), comes with such convincing proofs that if you do not have the appropriate scriptures, you may run out of your mind. It comes with such waves and force that defy gravity, till you call on heaven for help to stop it.

Those who are risen with Christ must be committed to praising Him, or doing warfare upon their beds therefore as counseled in Isaiah 42:11-12: *"...let the inhabitants of the rock sing, let them shout from the top of the mountains. Let them give glory unto the LORD, and declare his praise in the islands."*

You must be willing to do this, because you are one of the inhabitants of the rock (Christ). You are in Him and He dwells also in you. Therefore, the kingdom of heaven must suffer violence, and the violent should take it by force (Mathew 11:12).

Not taking guard over your thoughts in praise, worship or meditation is the worst mistake you can make. Watch how you go to bed. The devil is already waiting for you there whether you believe it or not. And so also is God. Resist the plan of the devil to engage your minds negatively, and strategically win the battle over your mind upon your bed.

When you allow the enemy to oppress your mind with evil thoughts, you are living carelessly, and living carelessly is a sin:

"Tremble with fear and stop sinning; think deeply about this, when you lie in silence on your beds. Offer the right sacrifices to the LORD, and put your trust in him." - Psalm 4:4-5 GNT

The Lord expects consistent resistance, not compromise. Think deeply about your challenges when you lie silently in bed, and trust the Lord to help you. Cast not away your confidence, which has a great recompense of reward (Hebrews 10:35). but *"Offer the right sacrifices..."*

The right sacrifices are prayer, praise, thanksgiving, and worship (Psalm 50:14, 23). Do strategic prayer and praise battle at midnight like Paul and Silas did (Acts 16:25). These men had every reason to breakdown, and engage in pity party, yet they chose to be joyful in glory. No matter your situation, choose joy above sorrow, and let the peace of God reign in your heart. Call on God, lie down and sleep, and do not be afraid of whether God will sustain you (Psalm 3:4-6).

Furthermore, Glory in the covenant promises of God, stand with him in absolute trust and confidence in His word, and let the devil know that you believe those promises. Let him know you are aware of the fact that every situation has an expiry date (Jeremiah 46:17). Also mention that the covenant of life you have with God carries with it hope of deliverance from all troubles, and He is your hiding place (Psalm 32:7). Many may be your afflictions, but God has promised to deliver you from them all; all you need to do is cry aloud (Psalm 37:17, 19).

When His word is affirmed in meditation, and you praise Him for what He has done, what He is doing and what He would yet do then you are rejoicing in glory (Psalm 149:5)! Sing aloud on your bed, terminate the battles raging in your minds, and take control of your spiritual atmosphere as you rejoice *"...in hope, patient in tribulation, and continuing steadfastly in prayer."* - Romans 12:12

You are God's witnesses to know, believe and understand these things (Isaiah 43:10). Do not be strangers to God's promises; you are His children and the apple of His eyes. He will neither leave you, nor forsake you (Hebrews 13:5). There is hope for the righteous, therefore in all things give thanks.

But many who do not know what to do suffer needlessly as people without hope, because there are no interpreters in their lives. Interpreters are scarce, they are one in a thousand, (Job 33:14-26). Your case should have been solved if only there were interpreters in your life. It is also clear that it is only if you, who need to benefit from the gifts of interpreters, avail yourself of the divine benefits made available to you, that you will find respite. Yet the Bible confirms in Isaiah 30:15b:

"...But you would not."

I pray you will not be part of this ignorant crowd; there is a way out of trouble if only you can seek Him.

What if you find it personally difficult to sing aloud, resist the devil with scriptures and do warfare on your own? That's okay for the moment, but make use of available kingdom resources on compact disks (CDs). Get hold of some and sing along as you cry out to God. Rip or store them on your computer hard drive if you have one, and make sure you listen to a series of music, audio

Bible or messages that inspire you at your bedside when you sleep and wake up.

I have for example on my Laptop and Tablet a series of music tracks, audio Bible and messages that play continuously till I choose to stop them from playing. Do the same in your car as you go to and fro to work, church or wherever you go. I daily enjoy a bank of mixed music, audio scriptures, and messages that richly load my mind positively. As I sing, and pray along, my mind is enriched.

When I reflect or meditate, I allow it to play in the background, and my thoughts are brought under subjection. I have done this for many years, and I see my wife and children doing the same. Do whatever is best for you, and cut off the satanic intruder from your heart and mind. Watch over your mind gate!

Furthermore, get reading materials, books and devotionals to inspire you daily. Engage your mind with testimonies of others who have fought and won the battles of life. Be selective in your book choices, making sure they meet your current and future needs. This is because you are a product of what you read, or what you read influences what you turn out to become. Therefore, buy books on Christian growth or growing in relationship with Christ, prayer, spiritual warfare, faith, handling common issues of life, meditation or reflections, gifts of the spirits and ministry gifts etc. Rich kingdom materials are also available on-line. Read wide and be empowered with the knowledge of truth, and be of good cheer, for He has overcome the world (John 16:33). Those who read lead.

Beloved, don't be afraid of the enemy, but confront it. The situation you face is not as bad as you think, therefore, settle it in your heart to keep watch over your mind gate. As you sing on your bed in challenging times, you cause your bed to become shorter, and your covering cloth narrower - (Isaiah 28:20). This means growth because when your bed is shorter and covering cloth narrower heaven resizes them without your asking.

A growing believer, is a one who is aglow in God - a shining light who cannot be hidden, and who as well walks in the path of light (Proverbs 4:18). Hannah, the mother of Samuel understood this fact so well, so every year she replaces the coat of Samuel, because she expects him to grow as he worships the Lord (1 Samuel 2:18-19).

God grows whatever He creates. That was the reason why after Samson's hair was shaved, it began to grow again and his strength was restored (Judges 16:21-22). Your glory can return so don't lose hope (Isaiah 60:1). He also grows whatever faith that is nurtured in Him, that was why the children of Israel grew in blessings from sacks to wagons and asses (Genesis 45:21-24).

Concerning growing in Christ, one needs to nurture his faith. Permit me to quote Rick Warren's insight on this subject. **"Christlikeness is nurtured by:**

- believing through worship (giving)
- belonging through fellowship (sacrifice)
- becoming through discipleship (surrendered life)

Looking closely at Psalm 149:5 further, it reads *"...let them sing aloud upon their beds."* Let me reiterate the fact again that do not go to bed with your mind floating, occupy it with deep reflections of His goodness that should end in thanksgiving and praise. When I do not sing aloud upon my bed, I do in the quietness of my heart in meditation, in order not to disturb my wife. Beyond singing aloud upon your bed, the next verse connects you to warfare.

"Let the high praises of God be in their mouth, and a two edged sword in their hands;" - Psalm 149:6

High praises in their mouth and two-edged sword (the word of God ref: Hebrews 4:12) in their hands. As you do you must declare who you are, what you want, and what God is able to do for you to stop the devil. The combination of high praises and the formidable Word of God is a strategic weapon of war deployed:

"To execute vengeance upon the heathen, and punishment upon the people; To bind their kings with chains, and their nobles with fetters of iron; To execute upon them the judgment written: this honor have all his saints, Praise ye the Lord." - Psalm 149:7-9

Even though you are commanded to offer high praises with two-edged sword in your hands to execute vengeance upon the heathen and punishment upon the people, it is not you that will carry it out, it is the Lord. He will join you in the battle because: *"...he taketh pleasure in his people, he will beautify the meek with salvation."* - Psalm 149:4. Therefore, labor to enter into this rest for: *"There remaineth...a rest for the people of God."* - Hebrews 4:9

Go boldly to the throne of grace that you may obtain mercy and find grace to help in the time of need (Heb 4:11, 15-16). This is the basic reason why He gave that command to offer high praises. He sows in you the thoughts of what to do, and gives the grace to carry it out (Psalm 84:11). If you know the benefit of being God's friend, you would do everything to please Him. The Psalmist declares:

"Happy is he that hath the God of Jacob for his help, whose hope is in the Lord." - Psalm 146:5

The condition for continuous help is to put your trust and hope for the best through Him. Don't *"...put your trust in princes or in the son of man in whom there is no help."* (v3). If the son of man helps you, it is because God empowers or enables him to do so. So do not shift your trust from God to man who will perish (v4). The master plan of God when He commanded you to offer higher praises is to get you to agree to what He wants to do. He is the one who in actual fact executes judgment on your behalf.

"Happy is he that hath the God of Jacob for his help...Which executeth judgment for the oppressed..." (v5, 7)

God is mindful of your situation, no matter the level of bondage you are in, He wants to deliver you. Not only that, He also wants to provide for your needs at the same time. He is the one who *"..... giveth food to the hungry."*

Furthermore, the Psalmist hits the high point and declares in the same verse *"...The Lord looseth the prisoners."* It's not your high praise/sword that does it, it's God. Your high praise is the process that lets God arise to fight on your behalf. When you let Him, He will open *"...the eyes of the blind..."* v8 and raise those *"...that are bowed down..."* He does not despise anyone. He turns to whosoever is willing to allow Him be God in his or her life.

"Behold, God is mighty, and despiseth not any: he is mighty in strength and wisdom." (Job 36:5).

Whatever side you turn to Him in truth and righteousness, He will work with you. He will not allow the wicked to take your place, but He *"...giveth right to the poor."* (v6) In addition, we see the divine dynamics and benefits of being with God or on the side of God. Furthermore in Job 36:7-14 we see the promises of God fully itemized:

"He withdraweth not his eyes from the righteous: but with kings are they on the throne; yea, he doth establish them for ever, and they are exalted." -v7

Note that amongst other benefits, God's plan is to establish and exalt you. And if there are resistance to His plans for your lives because of satanic bondages or afflictions, He is willing to reveal to you the root cause of your transgression, that you may return to Him, and through His mercies escape from the wicked.

"And if they be bound in fetters, and be holden in cords of affliction; Then he sheweth them their work, and their transgressions that they have exceeded. He openeth also their ear to discipline, and commandeth that they return from iniquity." (Job 36:8-10)

Deliverance from bondage is based on the willingness to obey, and serve Him in truth and righteousness. If they do, they: *".... shall spend their days in prosperity, and their years in pleasures.*

But if they obey not, they shall perish by the sword, and they shall die without knowledge." (Job 36:11-12)

It is, however, unfortunate, that the hypocrites do not take advantage of this divine benefit. They fall into the trap and die before their time. They lose the blessings of the kingdom and spend their years in hardship, yet the greatest desire of God is to deliver the poor in his affliction, because he delights in them.

But the hypocrites in heart heap up wrath: ***"...they cry not when he bindeth them. They die in youth, and their life is among the unclean. He delivereth the poor in his affliction, and openeth their ears in oppression."*** (Job 36:13-15)

Note verse 15, this is who our God is - a loving or doting Father, who desires to see you set free from all forms of bondage. He will do everything and anything to see you set free, if you cooperate with Him. Many do not understand this and they lose the benefit of His fatherhood. Job 36:16 best puts this across to us:

"Even so would he have removed thee out of the strait into a broad place, where there is no straitness; and that which should be set on thy table should be full of fatness."

But you suffered the pains of the ungodly because you refuse to cooperate with Him. Beloved, return to the Lord, and enjoy His blessings because it is in returning and rest that you shall be saved; and in quietness and confidence shall be your strength (Isaiah 30:15).

Going back to our text in Psalms 149:9 we read that the purpose of God in requesting us to offer high praises is:

"To execute upon them the judgment written:"

Which judgment, when was this judgment written, and what actually inspired it? The judgment of the Lord, and He declared it first in the Garden of Eden against the devil. In addition, the vain rebellion described in Psalm 2:1-3, which was a deliberate affront against the Lord, and His anointed, and God's immediate response to it, is also an example of His judgment written (Psalm 2:4-9). Apostle Peter interprets the word *"anointed"* in Psalm 2:2 correctly as *"His Christ"* in Acts 4:26. The full text is quoted below:

"Why do the heathen rage, and the people imagine a vain thing? The kings of the earth set themselves, and the rulers take counsel together against the Lord, and against his anointed, saying, 'Let us break their bands asunder, and cast away their cords from us." - Psalm 2:1-2

The four categories of people heathen, people, kings and nobles mentioned above are Horns of the Gentiles. The reference to the Horns of the Gentiles is first mentioned in Zechariah 1:21, however, we see them first introduced as a functional deadly group in Psalm 2:1-3. Their modus operandi is to break asunder the band of God's children, and cut their cords from them (We will discuss more about them in Chapter 3).

God's response to these horns was that of laughter, and He reminded these miscreants that He has set His king on His holy hill of Zion (v6). Furthermore, I will declare the decree of my empowerment, and the mandate I have to destroy (v9), therefore be wise O ye kings, and serve God in fear (v10-11). Needless to remind you that the downfall of these kings, and others began from their vain thoughts, just like Lucifer's as we read in Isaiah 14:12-13:

"How art thou fallen from heaven, O Lucifer...For thou hast said in thine heart I will ascend into heaven..."

When people's thoughts begin to go wild, watch out their downfall is close by. No wonder the Bible warns us:

"Keep thy heart with all diligence; for out of it are the issues of life." - Proverbs 4:23

Your heart or mind is a battleground, so be on your watch! Every battle you fight begins and ends in your mind. A person is shaped by his thoughts, and he is controlled for life whether negatively or positively. Proverbs 23:7 confirms this fact, that **"...as (a man) thinketh in his heart, so is he:..."** Therefore when you subject your heart and mind daily to a combination of praise and the word, declaring the promises of God without reservation, you initiate invisible battles in the heavens.

Whether you take the initiative to do so or not, the devil is waiting in the wings to do likewise. So why allow him to initiate the usual day or night battles against you when you can pre-empt him. All you need do is rest on your bed through praise. It's an unusual rest, but you need it to survive. If you do not have this rest you can never regain or renew strength, and it is those who wait on this command that will renew their strength (Isaiah 40:31). It is a strategic level warfare that you must intentionally fight, as you watch the gates of your hearts and minds, lying on your beds. You must be ready at all times with the word of life accompanying it. Beloved, let your prayer be:

"Return to your rest O my soul..." (Psalm 116:7-8).

"And therefore will the Lord wait, that he may be gracious unto you." (Isaiah 30:18-21).

"He that hath mercy on you will lead you, and guide you, so that you'd not suffer hunger and thirst in the land." (Isaiah 49:10).

When you return to him and rest through praise, giving thanks and worship, you will grow spiritually because:

"There remaineth ....a rest for the people of God" - Hebrews 4:9

Let us labor therefore to enter into that rest, by going boldly to the throne of grace, that we may obtain mercy and find grace to help in the time of need. (Heb 4:11, 15-16). It is in returning and rest that you can be saved, and in quietness and confidence that you can renew your strength (Isaiah 30:15; Jeremiah 30:10-11).

Let us conclude this chapter with the reflections of Joni Eareckson Tada, who caught the revelation of her bed as a formidable altar of praise and intercession.

Before You Begin
Thoughts from Joni Eareckson Tada

It was the summer of 1984 and I was catching up with an old friend over lunch. When she asked me about my journey with the Lord Jesus, I smiled and replied, **"I am convinced there's so much more to know, so much more to enjoy and understand about the Lord, and I've been asking Him to show me how to go deeper."**

My friend grinned and said, **Joni, I just happen to have something that may be an answer to your prayer.** She then pulled out of her handbag a copy of The Hour That Changes the World.

At first I was skeptical. It was such an unpretentious-looking little book. After I read it, however, I realized its insights and directives were just what I needed. The following week I made a copy of the page with the prayer plan, asked my husband to tape it to my bedroom wall unit, and then every night I dived into praise and waiting, confession and Scripture praying, watching, intercession, and all the rest. Little did I know that I was embarking on the most marvelous, awe-inspiring adventure of my Christian walk.

From that time on, **my bed became an altar of praise**. As a quadriplegic I cannot sit in my wheelchair too long, and I used to resent the early-to-bed routine. **But when I began to see my bed as a prayer platform, when I realized that lying down gave me a "looking-up" position** (a great prayer stance!), I started to look forward to 8:30 P.M.

The hours I spent communing with the Lord Jesus catapulted me into a whole new dimension of joy in the Lord.

Joni Eareckson Tada
Agoura Hills, California

(Eastman, D. (2002). The hour that changes the world. Grand Rapids, MI: Chosen).

What an incredible insight through personal experience! Her bed became the altar of Praise, and this experience catapulted her into a new dimension of joy in the Lord - singing aloud upon her bed (Psalm 149:5).

Furthermore, when she began to see (by revelation) her bed as a prayer platform, and realized that lying down gave her a **"looking-up"** position of Psalm 121:1 (a great prayer stance!), she started to look forward to 8:30 P.M. - the hour that changed her world, and her mission! What about you?

3
CHAPTER

The Horns of the Gentiles

"Then lifted I up mine eyes, and saw, and behold four horns. And I said unto the angel that talked with me, What be these? And he answered me, These are the horns which have scattered Judah, Israel, and Jerusalem. And the Lord showed me four carpenters. Then said I, What come these to do? And he spake, saying, These are the horns which have scattered Judah, so that no man did lift up his head: but these are come to fray them, to cast out the horns of the Gentiles, which lifted up their horn over the land of Judah to scatter it." - Zechariah 1:18-21

Background

In order for the Church to maintain her supremacy as a formidable army of believers raised to confront the hordes of darkness, she needs to be aware of the forces she is fighting against. The horns of the Gentiles are a gathering of evil entities that we must know about their operations in the land, and in the lives of people. These collections of evil entities, terrible in mien and disposition, only concentrate their attacks on the nation and its power base.

Their Operations and Manifestations

The horns of the Gentiles are territorial, and always corporate in their operations. They are very effective in their collective assault against their targeted victims, because they work as a team. Very vicious and audacious in their operations that they dared to gather *"...together against the Lord, and against his Christ."* - Act 4:26

These class of evil entities operate in mass visitation against their victims, forcing them to display uniform type of bondage i.e. collective captivity. You see a whole nation, community or family bound by the chains of alcoholism, immorality and poverty - these evil horns are behind it. They rule from the highest to the lowest and none is free from their hold, except one renewed in the spirit of Christ. The job specifications of the Horns, as we see in our introductory text, are to:

    i)   scatter Judah (the kingly tribe);
    ii) scatter Israel (the nation)
    iii) and scatter Jerusalem (the spiritual capital).

What is the purpose of the scattering? So that no man could lift up his head, make meaningful headway in life, or remain desperately limited. When you look deeply at what is going on here you wonder in resignation, what is left after they are done?

Are you surprised that the ruling tribes in many nations seem not to know what they are doing? No sane decision is made, and no forthright move is made to make things better, because they are under influences beyond their control. They assume power with good intentions, and when they begin to operate it's like scattered brains at work. Leadership does not see eye to eye even on basic issues obvious to common man. Why? Their brains and minds have been spiritually and collectively scattered.

The nation is not better. Nations receive the kind of leaders they deserve most of the time. In fact, some instead of condemnation, give insane commendations for the worst kind of government policies ever enacted. And because the tool of power - the media are available to them, they do worse damage to the nation than anyone could ever have imagined.

The Spiritual men possessing spiritual capital also get involved in the fray. These men clothe with renewed spirit, and new garment, who ought to know better, are forced to take obviously humiliating positions, just to be politically correct, that the Lord who called them into His service would never approve of. They are easily swept off their feet by the subtle manifestations of this **"logic scattering"** forces of darkness.

Specifically, the horns of the Gentiles carry out the following operations in the land. They:

   i)   make sure nobody excels or grows
   ii) cause instability in the kingly tribe
   iii) disrupt God's divine plan for Jerusalem (Christian homes) through inexplicable divisions and affect the house of God (the Church) negatively by making believers desire to be desperately like the world.

The power of the Church has been seriously diminished because the yardstick of success in the Church is how much of material acquisition you can flaunt. It is a mad race for greatness, championed by some Church leadership, who do nothing else but talk about how much their faith have made them rich. Self image is projected instead of self worth. What is the difference?

Self image is outward adorning of self to create an impression of who and what we are not! That is, the inauthentic self. Self worth, on the other hand, is revealed when the divine seed of life received in Christ is nurtured through the watering of His word in our inner man, and it continues to bear the fruits of godly character.

Sometimes truth is presented on the wings of half-truth. Believers are not told the true principles required to make faith work. Such as faith only works by love (Gal 5:6), and it is important to seek God first rather than His blessings (Matthew 6:33). They are not told that without faith it is impossible to please Him (Hebrews 11:6). They do not emphasize the fact that a lot of patience with painful obedience to God's word are required to make faith work. They are not made to understand that, it is as many as are led by the Spirit of God that are the sons of God (Rom 8:14); and if you are not led by the Spirit, you are none of His (Rom 8:9). Finally, they are not told that godly character is a key to answered prayer, because the Bible tells us:

*"**Follow peace with all men, and holiness without which no man can see the Lord.**"* - Hebrews 12:14

With all of the above principles missing in the lives of average Christians, who have been psyched up by their faith/prosperity preaching pastors, that they can become millionaires by acting in faith, they become easy preys to the forces of darkness. Of course when the route of faith results in frustrating delay, they will work it out through the manipulation of the flesh. They hereafter give highfaluting tales, which they tag testimonies, that have no bearing with the truth. By so doing they cause pain for the honest and God fearing ones who wonder why their own miracles have failed to happen. The book of Jude 1:12-13 describes them as: *"...spots in your feasts of charity, when they feast with you, feeding themselves without fear: clouds they are without water, carried about of winds; trees whose fruit withereth, without fruit, twice dead, plucked up by the roots; Raging waves of the sea, foaming out their own shame; wandering stars, to whom is reserved the blackness of darkness for ever."*

Spots or stains in our feasts of love, and clouds without water! They are intense in spreading their shameful lies, wandering about aimlessly and are never available to shine wherever they are needed - *"...they are wandering stars."*

Because they want to get rich quick, they fall into sin, and because the proceeds of sin are sweet, they get trapped in the suffocating grips of worldly allurement. Anything that controls your life has bewitched you. Witchcraft in its original definition is a python spirit that suffocates life out of its victims. Life has been snuffed out, and they remain a shadow of the believer they used to be. Believers watch out! Don't allow worldly riches prey on your soul.

The Horns of the Gentiles in Psalms

The Horns of the Gentiles are first clearly revealed to us in the Psalms 2:1-4. These specifically are the kings, the nobles, the heathen and the people. They do not work alone, and hence they are corporate in their operations and manifestations. In the same chapter, we see their audacity challenged by the Spirit of God, in order to make them know their place, and put a restraining embargo over them.

"Why do the heathen rage, and the people imagine a vain thing? The kings of the earth set themselves, and the rulers take counsel together, against the Lord, and against his anointed, saying, Let us break their bands asunder, and cast away their cords from us. He that sitteth in the heavens shall laugh: the Lord shall have them in derision."

The passage above depicts their arrogance and self conceited nature. We see here their vicious intentions against the Lord and His Christ. This also makes us to be aware that you have to be fully rooted in the Lord to deal with them. They are so subtle in their operations that you require depth of spiritual insight to discern them at work. When you observe their victims naturally, all may seem well from the outside, yet they are hopelessly dying on the inside.

Dealing with them requires consistent battle of high praises and the word of God. The early Church knew this very well, and therefore vehemently fought against them. This is the reason why they: *"...continued daily in one accord in the temple, and breaking bread from house to house."* (Acts 2:46).

We are also aware that Paul and Silas also exemplified this truth when at midnight they *"...prayed and sang praises unto God..."* (Acts 16:25) The Lord expects your battle with them to be ongoing, because they operate within the context of your daily routine in life. They are part and parcel of your daily activities, in so many ways that they easily know your vulnerabilities. You must be engaging against them in your thoughts, even as you lay on your bed to sleep. We read in Ps 149:5-6:

"Let the saints be joyful in glory; let them sing aloud upon their beds. Let the high praises of God be in their mouth, and a two edged sword in their hands."

Notice the connections between your bed and warfare, high praises and the two-edged sword (the word of God). This is simply because the powers of darkness are opportunistic warriors! They wait patiently till you are careless, weary or weak before they strike. Hence, God warns you ahead to be alert in high praises and the word, leaving nothing to chance.

As mentioned earlier, the early Church was always battle ready. They recognized from the word go that they were at war, hence it was not a layback Church, which solely depended on one miracle worker pastor to keep them fired-up as we have today. It was a purely a militant and fired-up triumphant Church.

Not only that, they recognized that they were at war with the horns of the Gentiles. Peter in Acts 4:25-27 referred to them, while praying with his company after being released from the hold (v23).

"Who by the mouth of thy servant David hast said, Why did the heathen rage, and the people imagine vain things? The kings of the earth stood up, and the rulers were gathered together against the Lord, and against his Christ. For of a truth against thy holy child Jesus, whom thou hast anointed, both Herod, and Pontius Pilate, with the Gentiles, and the people of Israel, were gathered together,"

The prophetic prayer said above inspired God to empower them to fight against their enemies. From the beginning of the Acts of the Apostles, it was from one battle to another, and God indeed granted them all round victory, no matter how terrible or vicious the battle was.

For example, notice that Peter mentioned Herod amongst those who gathered together. The Herod clan, for your information, was a thorn in the flesh of God's children from the birth of Christ, up till the birth of the early Church and beyond. The Holy Spirit specifically singled out for mentioning and judgment Herod Agrippa 1, the grandson of Herod the great (Luke 1:5) and the nephew of Herod the Tetrach (Luke 3:19). We saw in Acts 12:1-5 how he arrested and killed James, and proceeded to arrest Peter with the intention of killing him after Easter. But God waited for his cup to be full, and then an angel of the Lord smote him and worms ate him up because he failed to give God the glory (Acts 12:21-23).

It is salient to connect what happened here with Acts Chapter 6. What happened in Chapter 6:1-4 is a reminder of why the Church cannot afford to be distracted. The Church slept while the horns sowed seeds of division in the hearts of believers because of food. To resolve the problem the Apostles assigned prayer to themselves and left the whole Church to go into idleness:

"Wherefore, brethren, look ye out among you seven men of honest report, full of the Holy Ghost and wisdom, whom we may appoint over this business. But we will give ourselves continually to prayer, and to the ministry of the word." - Acts 6:3-4 (KJV)

Consequently, doors were opened for the spate of attacks believers suffered in the hands of their adversaries - beginning from Stephen (who was falsely accused - Acts 6:8-15). In Chapter 8:1-3, they pounced on the Church and scattered her and Paul *"... made harvoc of the Church..."* (Acts 8:3).

The consequence of the prayerlessness of the whole Church continued until Chapter 12, when James was arrested and killed because the Church failed to meaningfully pray for him. *"...Herod stretched forth his hands to vex certain (the leaders) of the Church. And he killed James the brother of John with the sword."* (v1)

Notice what inspired Herod to proceed and arrest Peter:

"And because he saw he pleased the Jews, he proceeded further to take Peter also." (v3)

The arrest of Peter opened the eyes of the leaders to know, that if they failed to pray, Peter would end up like James - dead by the sword of Herod. Therefore we read the encouraging response of the whole church in verse 5:

"Peter therefore was kept in prison but prayer was made without CEASING of the Church unto God for him.:"

Not only did God act on their prayer, He also acted on their earlier cry in Acts 4:30. Therefore, as they had asked, He *"...stretched forth His hands..."* against Herod and killed him. Herod was a Horn, hence God had to give him an unusual disgraceful death - worms ate him up! The death of Herod opened up a divine move of God in the Church. We read that *"...the word of God grew and the people multiplied...."* and secondly people began to fulfill their call or ministry (Acts 12:24-25).

You will observe here that there seems to be a contrast between the early Church and us. While they were prayerful and militant, we are docile and full of worldly pleasures. But if we must as the Church of Christ reclaim His Church in His name - we must first truthfully examine our knowledge and understanding of what we are called to do in the end-time Church.

We must be convincingly aware that we are called to be for signs and wonders (Isaiah 8:18). Also that we are not wanderers but wonders (Job 15:23; Jude 13). How much of this we know will determine how far we would fight. The book of Ecclesiastes 10:5-7 reveals an error that proceeds from the ruler. It is an evil under the sun. It speaks sadly of where the Church is today!

The ruler allowed evil to be carried out in his domain by putting aside wisdom *"which is profitable to direct"* (v10). He began with wisdom, and wisdom made him (Proverbs 2:10; Job 33:4). When he was made, he became comfortable and thereafter dug a pit of prayer-- lessness, and his hedge got broken (Ecclesiastes 10:8). Yet he fails to sharpen his dulled axe (v10; Hebrews 4:12), when necessary and keeps applying his old force to new symptoms without success. He becomes vulnerable, because of his weak defenses against the assault of his enemies. Hence, the serpent strikes, takes away his horse, and a servant begins to ride on it in dominating arrogance. The serpent can only bite without enchantment (v11 which is the Word Hebrews 4:12).

This is one reason you must study to show yourself approved unto God. God does not despise you when you fight back using His word, and not carnal weapons (Job 36:5-17). He promised to help (Matthew 16:18; 11:12). Therefore, as His witnesses let us acquire knowledge and understanding and fight (Is 43:10; Neh. 10:28-9). Let us equip ourselves and confront the enemy. Let us go to the foundation and root out the Horns of the Gentiles.

What Does Horn Represent?

1) Horns spiritually represent power (Psalm 92:10);
2) The ram's horn bears the anointing oil of empowerment - (I Samuel 16:1,13; I Kings 1:39);
3) It represents the voice of the prophetic and power when it is blown in battles it is called the Shofar (Joshua 6:4-8,13).
4) Horns can be exalted (I Samuel 2:1, 10) and they can also be cut off by God's power (Jeremiah 48:25)

But the horns of the Gentiles are much more in the negative sense, than what has been described above (Zechariah 1:21). They are deadly and you can only decipher them by revelation! To deal with them you must be able to lift up your spiritual eyes to heaven for deep insights into the mysteries of God (Zechariah 1:18; Psalm 121:1-2). Help must come from God to decipher who these formidable foes are, and what they are sent to do. Why is this so? It is because they operate at territorial or community, city or national levels. They are principalities (Ephesians 6:12).

For example fetish powers employ the use of horns in battles as we see in African movies. They are potent and backed by satanic powers. Similarly, the potency of the horns of the Gentiles enable them to scatter the ruling tribe; the nation and the Church. They make sure nobody excels or grows, and cause instability - coups, terror strikes, and social unrest in the nations. They also cause political division and crisis, disrupt God's divine plan, affect the house of God negatively, and scatter it.

From the above, we see that the devil has no new tricks what he did in the old (he scattered - Zechariah 1:19, 21), he repeated in the new: ***"...he scattered the Church throughout the regions of Judae and Samaria."*** - Acts 8:1

The Horns attacked God's servant Joshua the High Priest whose garment was filthy because his sons married strange wives (Zechariah 3:1-3; Ezra 10:18). But unknown to the devil at this time:

- They had repented by putting away the strange wives (Ezra 10:19)
- God had intervened for him (Zechariah 3:4-7)

We see them in their audacity attacking God in order to drive Him away from His house (the Church - Ezekiel 8:5-17). This is how audacious they are. Finally, they also attacked the city (Ezekiel 11:1-3).

What was God's response?

1) ***"Therefore I will also act in fury..."*** - (Ezekiel 8:18; 11:7-13,17)
2) ***"I will return to Jerusalem with mercies and my house shall be built in it."*** (Zechariah 1:16). God would have delivered the people earlier, but the heathen compounded their problem (Zechariah 1:12-16).

3) Because God is the builder of His Church, He stepped in to deliver His own (Matthew 16:18)
4) He says my line shall be stretched forth upon Jerusalem (Psalm 16:5-6)
5) He tells them what to do and say:

"Cry (pray) yet, saying Thus saith the Lord of hosts; "My cities through prosperity shall yet be spread abroad.
And the Lord shall yet comfort Zion, and shall yet choose Jerusalem.
(Zechariah 1:17).

Drawing from the scripture above, it is your responsibility to cry out aloud to God for Him to act. (We see an example in Ezekiel 36:37 where God waited on Israel to ask). In response to their cry in this passage, God sent four carpenters (intercessors) which represent corporate grace, to fray the horns, and cast them out (v21, Luke 3:9). This is exactly what we are called to do (Jeremiah 1:10). The horns of the wicked must be cut off and their arms broken (Psalm 75:10; Jeremiah 48:25). Do so till Jesus comes.

4

CHAPTER

The Spirit, the Word And the Power

"And behold I send the promise of my father upon you; but tarry ye in the city of Jerusalem, until ye be endued with power from on high." - Luke 24:49

Without any doubt the essential ingredient for victory in warfare, is God making His power available through the Word and the Spirit. This is the wisdom behind the Lord Jesus telling the disciples to wait for power *"...tarry ye in the city of Jerusalem, until ye be endued with power from on high."* - Luke 24:49

Power is very important to attain victory in spiritual warfare. This power is the strength that comes from above, not abroad as some will joke. When your power is dependent on God's strength, you're wise and the Bible calls you blessed:

"Blessed is the man whose strength is in thee..." - Psalm 84:5

You are called blessed because you are dependent on Him, relying on His every word and trusting Him with your life. Those who do get the reward of trusting Him - that's why they are blessed. It is also written earlier in the passage that these group of people will forever be praising Him for the results of His victories in their lives (Psalm 84:4). These are men who walk in the ways of men who have the hearts of turning impossible situations around. They prayed down rain over a dry valley and turned it to a well of water - *"...the rain also filleth the pools."* (Psalm 84:6)

These are men who have learnt the power of obedience, and its fruits. They have learnt to sit at the feet of the Master until he makes their enemies their footstools (Psalm 110:1-3). They have refused to struggle with the Lord when He makes them, against their own will, to lie down in green pastures for one basic reason - to restore their souls (Psalm 23:2). He thereafter leads *"...them in the paths of righteousness for his name's sake"* (v3). These are men who know how to die and live in Him, drawing unusual strength that the world can never give.

People can do whatever they will, but it is a matter of time. Like some do say **"Time will tell."** And indeed time really do tell. I remember the story of a young man who went with his grandfather to plant corn seedlings in the farm. This young man lacked discretion and was impatient. Against his grandfather's instructions to put just one corn seed into the mound, he sometimes put five, seven or ten as it met his hurried fancy.

The Old man kept asking him **"Son, are you sure you are putting one seed in each mound?"** His answer was always **"Yes Grandpa."** The Old man told him somehow I still feel your speed is somewhat dubious, yet the boy insisted that he was keeping to instruction. The Old man told him **"Time will reveal it."** He didn't understand until two weeks later when the result of his indiscretion, and deception sprung out of the ground for all to see. It was then that the reality of his bad judgment caught up with him. His grandfather had to do the work of replanting the shoots with accompanied knocks on his head.

The same is true of the disciples of Christ who were diligently taught by the Lord on what to do, but after several years they still struggled to connect with the vision. What went wrong? The word, the Spirit and power were missing. So what did the Lord do to put them in line with His vision, will or desire? He provided them with His Spirit, Word and Power. By these they became effective instruments in His hands. Let us begin with the experience of Peter.

A) Peter

Apostle Peter, sporting from his background as a tough fisherman, was a self assured and impulsive personality that bordered on arrogance. So when the Lord warned him of Satan's impending attack, instead of taking the word seriously, he began to argue just to prove he was a strong and faithful man.

"And the Lord said, Simon, Simon, behold, Satan hath desired to have you, that he may sift you as wheat: But I have prayed for thee, that thy faith fail not: and when thou art converted, strengthen thy brethren. And he said unto him, Lord, I am ready to go with thee, both into prison, and to death." - Luke 22:31-33

It is not possible to comprehend the works of the Spirit with the flesh. Yet Peter took the counsel lightly, in spite of the fact that the Lord:

"...said, I tell thee, Peter, the cock shall not crow this day, before that thou shalt thrice deny that thou knowest me." - Luke 22:34

He dragged his feet about the matter until he began to *"...follow afar off..."* (v54). When you jettison the word of life, and keep yourself shut out of the leading of the Spirit, you will lack the power to follow closely. Not only that, your chance of denying Him is very high, and that was exactly what he did. He lied to his accusers he never knew the Lord until the cock crew:

"And Peter said, Man, I know not what thou sayest. And immediately, while he yet spake, the cock crew. And the Lord turned, and looked upon Peter. And Peter remembered the word of the Lord, how he had said unto him, Before the cock crow, thou shalt deny me thrice. And Peter went out, and wept bitterly." - Luke 22:60-62

When the Lord turned back and looked at him, he had an encounter. He remembered what the Master said, went out and wept bitterly. A deep surge of remorse and repentance swept all over him. He was never going to be the same again thereafter. The experience totally changed the inward, and outward perceptions of Peter for good. He received the Word from the Lord, the Spirit at Pentecost and divine power began to manifest in him. The old impulsive, quick to act Simon died, and the renewed deliberate or intentional Peter was born. He became a changed man!

After this personal encounter with the Lord, we could see, a confident and knowledge-able Peter at Pentecost, demonstrating the presence of the Lord in his life and ministry. We could hear him confidently say at the gate beautiful:

"...Silver and gold have I none; but such as I have give I thee: In the name of Jesus Christ of Nazareth rise up and walk." - Acts 3:6

What a rare demonstration of divine knowledge, and God's presence at work. He knew what he had, and did not mince words about it. This was no more the timid and fearful Peter going about with sword, but one renewed by his experiencing the mercy and goodness of the Lord. He deserved to be punished for denying the Lord, yet God showed him mercy, worked with him and transformed his life. His growth in grace was so awesome that we gladly read that his shadow healed the sick:

"And believers were the more added to the Lord, multitudes both of men and women.) Insomuch that they brought forth the sick into the streets, and laid them on beds and couches, that at the least the shadow of Peter passing by might overshadow some of them." - Acts 5:14-15

Beyond Peter, what did Jesus do to the rest of the disciples to restore them? Remember they all forsook Him and fled (Mt 26:56)? Even when they waited for Him at the upper room, the doors were strictly shut because of the fear of the Jews. They were in a state of morbid fear, full of uncertainty and unsure of what the Master represented in their lives.

While they went through this restive season, the Lord showed up in several instances and settings, beginning at the road to

Emmaus. In His usual kindness, He made some landmark changes in their lives, that restored them back on track. The following changes are identified below. He opened their:

- Eyes (Luke 24:31)
- Hearts (Luke 24:32)
- Unto them the scriptures (Luke 24:32)
- Understanding (Luke 24:45)
- Heaven (Acts 1:9-10)

B) John the Baptist

John the Baptist as we read in the scriptures was baptized in the Holy Spirit right from his mother's womb (Luke 1:39-45), chosen to be a lonely voice in the wilderness, a forerunner of the Lord Jesus, and was located by God's word in the wilderness: **"...the word of God came unto John the son of Zacharias in the wilderness."** - Luke 3:2

For him to function effectively in his role as a lonely voice, he had to be filled with the Holy Spirit, and receive the word of life from heaven. Usually miracles are the magnet that attract people to the call of God, yet in John's case that was not so. People trooped to him in the wilderness despite this! What was the secret? The power of the spoken word. This power drew people to him with such compelling force that they could not resist. This was one reason why he could call the people vipers, and yet they continued going to him (Luke 3:7-14).

John the Baptist, like every man used of God was full of power by the Spirit of the Lord:

"But truly I am full of power by the spirit of the LORD, and of judgment, and of might, to declare unto Jacob his transgression, and to Israel his sin." (Micah 3:8)

Do not to undertake any assignment for God without receiving His Spirit, His Word and Power. If you do, you will endanger your life and the lives of the followers of Jesus you minister to. Putting aside this counsel would put you in the same predicament the sons of Sceva found themselves in Acts 19:13-16:

"...And the evil spirit answered and said, Jesus I know, and Paul I know; but who are ye? And the man in whom the evil spirit was leaped on them, and overcame them, and prevailed against them, so that they fled out of that house naked and wounded." (v15-16)

C) The Lord Jesus

Just like John encountered the word in the wilderness, so did the Lord Jesus while he was being baptized, and praying the Holy Spirit came down upon Him in form of a dove and affirmed Him as the only begotten of the Father:

"Now when all the people were baptized, it came to pass, that Jesus also being baptized, and praying, the heaven was opened, And the Holy Ghost descended in a bodily shape like a dove upon him, and a voice came from heaven, which said, Thou art my beloved Son; in thee I am well pleased." - Luke 3:21-22

In one full breath the Spirit, the Word and Power came upon the son of man in order to effectively carry out the assignment God had for Him:

"And Jesus being full of the Holy Ghost returned from Jordan, and was led by the Spirit into the wilderness," - Luke 4:1

"And Jesus returned in the power of the Spirit into Galilee: and there went out a fame of him through all the region round about. And he taught in their synagogues, being glorified of all." - Luke 4:14-15

In your Christian race the Spirit, the Word and Power must be present for you to operate as the violent one in order to take the Kingdom by force, and work out your salvation with fear and trembling.

5
CHAPTER

The Violent Takes it By Force

"And from the days of John the Baptist until now the kingdom of heaven suffereth violence, and the violent take it by force." - Matthew 11:12

The violent one is the believer who knows who he is, what he is called to do, and the power of God available to him. He is also aware that he is for a sign and wonder (Isaiah 8:18). He is well informed of the promises of God, and how faithful He is to His word. He also knows the plan of God to build His Church, and the gates of hell shall not prevail against it (Mt 16:18).

With that mindset or understanding he is ready to take what belongs to him, and the Church by force. He does not give the devil a breathing space to kill, to steal and to destroy. He knows that the only language Satan understands is force. He is a fighter, and willing battle axe in God's hand against the devil. We see this truth demonstrated in Elijah, whom the King sent captains of fifty to arrest in 2 Kings 1:10:

"And Elijah answered and said to the captain of fifty, If I be a man of God, then let fire come down from heaven, and consume thee and thy fifty. And there came down fire from heaven, and consumed him and his fifty."

He called down fire down twice, and used this weapon of mass destruction to roast a hundred and two men before God stopped him, and told him to go down and follow the last captain of fifty. God is the master strategist who orders the course of every battle, if you allow Him, He will guarantee your victory in every battle:

"And the angel of the LORD said unto Elijah, Go down with him: be not afraid of him. And he arose, and went down with him unto the king." - 2 Kings 1:15

In every spiritual battle we engage in, the violent one must be led by the Spirit at all times. He must have a vibrant worship, word, prayer, and fasting relationship with the Lord. He cannot afford to be an impulsive, and careless kind of a Christian. Or else he will depopulate the kingdom, by sending many potential souls to their early graves. The violent one must therefore, be diligent,

"...fervent in spirit; serving the Lord..." (Romans 12:11)

Paul and Silas were another good examples of the violent ones taking things by force. Psychologically speaking at that time, they could be excused for being discouraged, because of their incarceration, yet they chose to pray and praise God at midnight. Unlike Peter who at midnight slept, these ones chose to be fervent, and turned the battle to the gates of the enemy. Their fervency inspired God to show up in an earthquake, the foundations of the prison were shaken, all doors were opened, and every one's bands were loosed. (Acts 16:25-26).

If Paul and Silas had kept quiet in pity party, worse things could have befallen them, and they would not have gotten their victory. If they had not been spiritually violent, the Jailor, who witnessed the signs and wonder elicited by offering high praises unto God, would not have been saved with his family that day after he asked: **"...Sirs, what must I do to be saved?"** (v30).

Spiritual violence has its benefits, and we must pursue them. We are called to be as wise as serpent and cool as dove. To remain a dove alone is tantamount to committing strategic suicide, and dying before one's time. And to be a serpent all the time is to be an unkind, wicked, heartless and terrible believer void of compassion, and I doubt if such a person could ever please God.

To enjoy the blessings heaven has made available to you, you must violently possess them. The Lord Himself in Deut 2:24 commands us to fight in order to possess:

"Rise ye up, take your journey, and pass over the river Arnon: behold, I have given into thine hand Sihon the Amorite, king of Heshbon, and his land: begin to possess it, and contend with him in battle."

Whether you believe it or not this is the kingdom requirement, and God resist those who have chosen to remain weaklings in spite of His strength made available to them. He cannot tolerate the weak hearted who refuse, for the reason of fear, to contend with the enemy. In fact, God sees them as wasters of kingdom resources. He has called us to fight, and not to turn our backs at the enemy. For example, God rebuked Moses when he became confused in fear, and lost touch with what to do. He asked him:

"Why do you cry to me? Tell the children of Israel to go forward." - Exodus 14:15

Even though Moses cried aloud in prayer, God perceived it as confused and fearful cry. God knew what was going through his mind, even though he began very well, by declaring God's word and reassuring the people about what God would do to save them that day:

"And Moses said unto the people, Fear ye not, stand still, and see the salvation of the LORD, which he will shew to you to day: for the Egyptians whom ye have seen to day, ye shall see them again no more for ever. The LORD shall fight for you, and ye shall hold your peace." - Exodus 14:13-14

All God needed him to do after applying the word was for him to step out with the people and go forward in faith. But when Moses began to cry aloud in fear, God could not stomach it.

The same scenario played out in Micah, and the Holy Spirit responded to the fearful cry:

"Now why dost thou cry out aloud? is there no king in thee? is thy counsellor perished? for pangs have taken thee as a woman in travail. Be in pain, and labour to bring forth..." - Micah 4:9-10

Beloved you have the king of kings dwelling in you, and your counselor the Holy Spirit is not dead, He is alive inyou! So arise and deal with the enemies before they truncate your destiny. Don't wait till a witch kills you, and use you to testify during her conversion testimony - it would have been too late then to fight! The Second Epistle to the Thessalonians 1:6 tells us:

"...it is a righteous thing with God to recompense tribulation to them that trouble you:..."

The violent is expected to remove whatever obstacles may be in his way e.g. Samson removed the gate of the City to escape the attacks of his enemy:

"Then went Samson to Gaza, and saw there an harlot, and went in unto her.
And it was told the Gazites, saying, Samson is come hither. And they compassed him in, and laid wait for him all night in the gate of the city, and were quiet all the night, saying, In the morning, when it is day, we shall kill him.
And Samson lay till midnight, and arose at midnight, and took the doors of the gate of the city, and the two posts, and went away with them, bar and all, and put them upon his shoulders, and carried them up to the top of an hill that is before Hebron." - Judges 16:1-3.

Your enemies are not asleep; they are at work full time. So why are you asleep? Wake up! Confront all oppositions and manipulations of darkness against your rising. The violent ones take their blessings by force, and do not sit down expecting manna to fall from heaven. They shun excuses, but take appropriate actions to get their miracles by force. They force hopeless situations to change, and wait on God till they see their change come.

"If a man die, shall he live again? all the days of my appointed time will I wait, till my change come." (Job 14:14).

Every believer cannot be anything but otherwise - a violent warrior, fighting the fight of faith because from

"...... the days of John the Baptist until now the kingdom of heaven suffereth violence, and the violent take it by force." (Matthew 11:12)

The Lord in Matthew 16:18 to build His Church and the gates of hell shall not prevail against it. We are to respond to this challenge literally, and fight. We are called to be soldiers for Christ. A soldier is trained to fight and cannot afford to mess himself up with civil affairs of life - he must be strong to fight:

"Thou therefore endure hardness, as a good soldier of Jesus Christ." - 2 Timothy 2:3

What are the lessons here? Position yourself to be trained as a good soldier of Christ. Be strong in your worship, prayer, fasting, and word content. Be filled and full of the Holy Spirit richly, speaking in tongues to build up your holy faith, and be drunk in the spirit. Take heed to Paul's admonition, and be empowered to fight violently. Take the battles of life by force, and do not look back, as you continue to:

"Rejoice evermore. Pray without ceasing. In every thing give thanks: for this is the will of God in Christ Jesus concerning you. Quench not the Spirit. Despise not prophesyings. Prove all things; hold fast that which is good. Abstain from all appearance of evil." - 1 Thess. 5:16-22

6

CHAPTER

Possessing Divine Promises

"Rise ye up, take your journey, and pass over the river Arnon: behold, I have given into thine hand Sihon the Amorite, king of Heshbon, and his land: begin to possess it, and contend with him in battle. This day will I begin to put the dread of thee and the fear of thee upon the nations that are under the whole heaven, who shall hear report of thee, and shall tremble, and be in anguish because of thee." (Deut 2:24-25)

"And the Lord gave unto Israel all the land which he sware to give unto their fathers; and they possessed it, and dwelt therein." - (Josh 21:43)

The beauty of coming to the knowledge of the Lord, is the discovery of pleasant surprises He had packaged for us, as we journey along with Him in faith. The joyful things to observe as a person receives Jesus as Lord and Savior, are that He begins to do the following for the converted soul:

i)   He relieves his pain (Psalm 69:29 NIV),
ii) He reveal his virtues (Isaiah 33:6) and
iii) He releases his gifts (Isaiah 12:3).

These three things do not just happen automatically, it is a process we must be willing to walk through as we trust and obey Him. His promises are available for all to see, explore and enjoy. But the error in the Church is our ignorance on how it works. We assume

God would drop them on our laps. It does happen like that, you must arise and fight for it!

The journey to success requires you to do something in obedience to God's word. You must move within the framework of His leading to enjoy divine benefits. There is nothing in your life that God has not provided for. Nothing takes Him by surprise; He is in control of all situation. He has made adequate provisions through His promises for you to excel. But you must rise up to take possession. He has already given you and I the oppressor and his land, therefore, *"... begin to possess it, and contend with him in battle."* - Deut. 2:24

Nobody acquires a thing of value without contending for it. If anyone tells you He receives a thing of value without a fight, watch out, it is either fake, or someone acquired it on his behalf. Possessing divine possessions is a personal endeavor, which you must carry out. You must, like David, be willing to pursue, overtake and without fail recover all (I Samuel 30:8).

Beyond this, it is not sufficient to possess, you must be willing to prayerfully retain, maintain, and sustain by warding off the sporadic diabolical onslaught of evil ones. Many have possessed, but are unable to dwell in their possessions. Some labored to get good jobs, placements in college, husbands or homes and are later unceremoniously kicked out of their prized possessions.

When you lose your possession, it's not the devil's fault, it's yours. You need to be aware of the strategy of the devil - he never gives up what is taken from him! He will always come after you, until he is knocked out by a superior firepower. What this means is that you must spiritually equip yourself continually to ward off surprise attacks from the enemy's camp. You cannot afford to be careless or lethargic when dealing with the adversary. There are four strategies you must learn to adopt in order to keep that which God has given to you. These I call four levels of grace, or four power levels required for you to dwell in your possessions.

These are:

- Power to Ascend
- Power to Stand - (Psalm 24:3)
- Power to Abide
- Power to Dwell - (Psalm 15:1)

It takes grace or (power) to ascend His holy hill and remain steadfast there without the accuser of the brethren distracting you with relentless false accusations. Being able to remain *"...stedfast, unmoveable, always abounding in..." prayer is as a result of the Power to Stand."* (I Cor. 15:58). Not only do you require the power to having done all to stand (Eph 6:13); you also need the Power to Abide. It is when grace is given to abide, that you may be able to present a formidable argument against the kingdom of darkness.

Who can dwell?

Without mincing words Psalms 15:2-5 reveals to us those who can dwell on God's holy hill.

"He that walketh uprightly, and worketh righteousness, and speaketh the truth in his heart... He that doeth these things shall never be moved."

The Bible passage clearly gives us the reason why many fail to retain their place on mount Zion, the prayer mountain. The conditions required to dwell are vividly spelt out: - it is to keep His laws (Leviticus 26:3-13). His laws also are not grievous, but they help a person to walk in the path of life. His covenant of peace (Ezek 34:25-30), is also available to guarantee your rest roundabout.

"And now the LORD your God hath given rest unto your brethren, as he promised them: therefore now return ye, and get you unto your tents, and unto the land of your possession,..." - Joshua 22:4

This promise of God is true for all those who repose their trust in Him. We are aware that King Asa enjoyed peace and rest, as he grew in the presence of the Lord. He found rest at a time when turbulence, and chaos was the order of the day. God gave him rest because he sought God when it mattered most, and God prospered him in all he laid his hands upon.

"And he built fenced cities in Judah: for the land had rest, and he had no war in those years; ...because we have sought the LORD our God, we have sought him, and he hath given us rest on every side. So they built and prospered." - 2 Chron 14:6-7

The reward of obedience to God's word, and His loving-kindness are available to as many as are willing to walk with Him, no matter the cost. Obedience is costly, if you must know. but the reward far outweighs the cost!

Like in popular saying: **"If education is costly, try ignorance."** Similarly, **"If obedience is costly, try disobedience."**

Because of His loving-kindness that is better than life, your covenant of peace from Him is secured. Many turbulent things may happen around you but as he promised *"...my kindness shall not depart from thee, neither shall the covenant of my peace be removed, saith the LORD that hath mercy on thee."* (Isaiah 54:10)

In spite of the challenges of life, He will establish you in righteousness (v14). What seems to you to be a nightmare will turn out to be a time of celebration, and you shall *"...be far from oppression; for thou shalt not fear: and from terror; for it shall not come near thee."* (v14) You shall not be put to shame (Is 61:7-9), and none of your enemies would be able to stand before you, they shall all fall and never rise again (Deut 11:25; 33:11; I Sam 30:8-18).

And this shall be your testimony:

"There failed not ought of any GOOD thing which the Lord had spoken unto the house of Israel - ALL CAME TO PASS. - Joshua 21:43

7
CHAPTER

When the Righteous Gather Fire Falls

"When the people are gathered together, and the kingdoms, to serve the Lord." (Psalm 102:22)

"For where two or three are gathered together in my name, there am I in the midst of them." (Matthew 18:20 KJV)

The reward received for every gathering of Christians is God's manifest presence, and release of power. When two or three gather in His name, He shows up as promised in Matthew 18:20. Even though He is ever present with us, He evidently manifests Himself when we need His help such as in the case of Paul and Silas in Acts 16:25-26. In a nutshell, when He shows up, glorious things happen; He shows up to turn sadness to joy, and sorrow to laughter! One of His preoccupations is to hear the cries of those imprisoned, loose the bonds of wickedness, and set free those appointed to die. He does it by declaring the name of Jesus as the redeemer, deliverer, provider and healer. In fact, these are few of the several reasons He came as we read in Psalm 102:19-21.

"For he hath looked down from the height of his sanctuary; from heaven did the LORD behold the earth; To hear the groaning of the prisoner; to loose those that are appointed to death; To declare the name of the LORD in Zion, and his praise in Jerusalem;"

God's desire always, is to give you unending laughter. This should not surprise you because His word tells us that in His presence is the fullness of joy, and at his right hand are pleasures for ever more (Psalms 16:11). He wants us to be partakers of this joy, because he takes pleasure in His own. This is who God is - a compassionate and caring father.

Do you know that God's plan for you is to enjoy laughter or miracles on a daily basis? The scripture unapologetically declares **"He daily loads us with benefits..."** (Psalm 68:19). In Psalm 103:2 the Psalmist encourages us not to forget **"...all his benefits:"** and goes on from verses three through fourteen to give us a rundown list of the benefits.

It is important however, for you to know that divinely inspired laughter does not come by accident. You have to position yourself for it, and also must be expectant. When God shows up he wants to see the following before He moves in your lives.

1). A Right Heart

There must be a preparation of the HEART just as we read in Judges 5:15b that **"...the divisions of Reuben there were great searchings of heart."** They re-evaluated their positions and made necessary adjustments for the better. When God comes He communicates His presence through your HEART! Hence the first thing He does, when He comes is to look into your heart to see if He can find a place to dwell in. If He does not find a place in your heart, He quietly takes His leave.

Why is your heart so important? It is because it is with the heart man believes unto righteousness (Rom. 10:10). The encounter of Samuel and Eliab is a good case in point. As far as Samuel was concerned Eliab was the man, but God rejected him because of his heart. **"...But the LORD said unto Samuel, Look not on his countenance, or on the height of his stature; because I have refused him: for the LORD seeth not as man seeth; for man looketh on the outward appearance, but the LORD looketh on the heart."** 1 Samuel 16:7

The question before you now is **"How pure is your heart or how broken are you?"** Honestly examine and meditate on the following scriptures for your help.

"Blessed are the pure in heart: for they shall see God." - Matthew 5:8
"The Lord is nigh unto them that are of a broken heart; and saveth such as be of a contrite spirit." - Psalm 34:18
"The sacrifices of God are a broken spirit: a broken and a contrite heart, O God, thou wilt not despise." - Psalms 51:17 (KJV)

Having examined these scriptures, you will agree with me, this is a serious business. You must be broken and must possess a contrite heart for Him to visit you. The quotation below better highlights the subject on hand.

"A world that celebrates success does not see value in broken things. But God brings beauty out of brokenness. For the plant to rise from the soil, the seed must be broken. For a chick to come out and experience outer life the shell must be broken. For a baby to come out of the womb, the water must break. Even a thorough bread horse must be broken, to serve its owner without harm.

Through brokenness God strips us of self sufficiency to the extent that we have no strength left to fix ourselves. It happened to Paul on the road to Damascus, and after reevaluating the religious activity he once boasted about, he called it "dung." (Phil 3:8). When God is all you have - God is all you need! Bottom line: God's power is reserved for those who have given up trying to do it in their own strength, or to accomplish it for their own ends!" - Anonymous

God's Solution to Evil Heart

a) God's plan is to give you *"... one heart, and one way, that they may fear me for ever, for the good of them, and of their children after them:"* (Jeremiah 32:39). He is giving YOU a new heart for your good, and that of your children. Therefore, guard your heart jealously, and be not deceived:

"Take heed, brethren, lest there be in any of you an evil heart of unbelief, in departing from the living God. But exhort one another daily, while it is called To day; lest any of you be hardened through the deceitfulness of sin." - Hebrews 3:12-13

b) God wants you to get acquainted with him in a heart to heart relationship. This is one and only way to have a right heart in your thinking towards Him. When you start a heart to heart relationship with the Lord, in praise worship and word meditation, He does everything to grow your faith and give you an inheritance among those that are sanctified (Acts 20:32). The book of Job 22:21 therefore encourages you to:

"Acquaint now thyself with him, and be at peace: thereby good shall come unto thee."

It is through acquainting yourself with Him that your peace will come. He is the Prince of Peace, and being at peace is a settled command from above to all who put their trust in Him. God keeps them in perfect peace because their mind is stayed on Him through trusting Him (Isaiah 26:3).

c) He desires that you lay His law in your heart in meditation, because as a man *"...thinketh in his heart, so is he..."* (Proverbs 23:7). The fastest way to grow in Christ is through ruminating on God's word. Hence we are encouraged by Job to:

"Receive, I pray thee, the law from his mouth, and lay up his words in thine heart..." - Job 22:22

d) God seeks for a heart that is willing to return to Him in repentance and absolute surrender. If this is genuinely done, then the Lord shall be your defense and your prosperity will be assured. *"If thou return to the Almighty, thou shalt be built up, thou shalt* *put away iniquity far from thy tabernacles. Yea, the Almighty shall be thy defence, and thou shalt have plenty of silver."* - Job 22:23, 25

The result is that you will have your delight in the Lord, and find joy or satisfaction in prayer. You will also pray effectively and also issue decrees with answers following. Therefore, your confidence in God and His word will increase. Your unshakable faith will make you take a stand on the side of God no matter what you see to the contrary (Job 22:26-30).

Whether you believe it or not. Your miracle is tied to your REPENTANCE from evil heart of unbelief in departing from the living God (Hebrews 3:13). Job also confirms and reemphasizes this fact in Job 11:13,15:

"If thou prepare thine heart, and stretch out thine hands toward him; ... then shalt thou lift up thy face without spot; ..."

Impure or evil heart is one reason why our laughter or miracle has eluded us. It is those with pure hearts that will receive the blessing and righteousness from our God. The Psalmist in Psalm 24:3 asks us a pertinent question: *"Who shall ascend into the hill of the Lord?..."* The answer still remains the same the one with *"...a pure heart;..."*

A Christian who neglects the work of the Holy Spirit in his heart is like a lamp that is not plugged in. Hence, he'll not bring forth light, but remain in darkness because there is no power supply (Phil 2:13). This one will not succeed as we read in Zechariah 4:6 (GW).

"Then he replied, "This is the word the Lord spoke to Zerubbabel: You won't {succeed} by might or by power, but by my Spirit, says the Lord of Armies."

Further to this, let us read below a reflection on true circumcision, and how our heart is deeply involved.

"He alone can deal effectually with our heart, and take away its carnality and pollution. To make us love God with all our heart

and soul is a miracle of grace which only the Holy Ghost can work. We must look to the Lord alone for this and never be satisfied with anything short of it." (Faith's Checkbook)

2. Faith

The second crucial thing He wants to see is your faith - God's kind of faith. This is important because the just shall live by faith, and *"...without faith it is impossible to please him:..."* (Hebrews 11:6) Yet many have unknowingly ignored the counsel of Paul in Eph. 6:16 to take up the shield of faith to their pain and vulnerability. They therefore suffer needless attacks of Satan on their faith.

Satan's arrows can't penetrate a heart that's pure, saturated in the WORD and fortified by faith. That's why Jesus told Peter *"I have prayed for you, that your faith should not fail."* - Luke 22:32

You better believe it, it is your faith that is under attack when Satan comes after you in every situation you have ever faced. Do everything possible to always nurture or feed your faith. Without it you have no sustenance in life, you are empty, shallow and ready to be discarded. No wonder Jesus warns, *"Have faith in God."* (Mark 11:22).

Note, he didn't just say, **"Have faith in something bigger than yourself."** No, he said, **"Have faith in God."** He tells you to do so because He knows full well that, that is the basis for living. Without faith you can never amount to anything either in God or with men. Where strength is lacking, faith has failed or is not there in the first place. Faith builds the power from within, and enables you to do exploit in Him, but you must deliberately wait on Him to build your faith and strength:

"He gives power to the weak, and to those that have no might He increases strength." - Isaiah 40:29

God gives each of us a *"measure of faith"* (Romans 12:3 NKJV). But Jude says you must develop it by *"building yourself up in your most holy faith,"* (Jude 20)

Faith under attack is faith under construction. It is in the battles of life that you discover whether you have nurtured faith or neglected faith. To enjoy nurtured faith, or faith that endures you must believe he is alive as you diligently seek him. The Epistle to the Hebrews 11:6 broken down below, reveals to us the basis of faith. It reiterates the fact that:

a) he that cometh to God must believe that he is,
b) and that he is a rewarder of them
c) that diligently seek him."

Be willing to work on your faith and beware of those who say, **"it can't be done."** Refuse to let the word **"impossible"** stop you. Jesus said, *"With God all things are possible."* (Luke 18:23) The problem of many believers is that we easily succumb to believing for too little than believing for too much. With God, your believing must be bigger than you, if not it is not God. Anything that man can do for you why waste time bothering God about it.

Vision is essential for your survival, without it you are an empty shell. And a God-given vision is conceived by faith, sustained by prayer and fueled by God's word in order to make the desired impact. It is not just about what you can do, but what God can do with your life when it is fully surrendered to Him. *"Where there is no vision, the people perish."* - Proverbs. 29:18. Therefore believe God for great things!

3. Follow Peace With All Men.

The third thing God looks for is your relationship with others. Do you pay evil for evil or are you: *"....an example of the believers in word, in conversation, in charity, in spirit, in faith, in purity."* (I Tim 4:12)

To have God move on your behalf, you must follow peace with all men (Heb 12:14). But some Christians have short fuses, while some are desperately angry, vengeful, and un-forgiven. These ones are so deep that they specialize in keeping ancient grudges. Issues that ought to be long forgotten are restored, renewed or refurbished, and presented as fresh menu serve to as many tale hearers willing to listen to their garbage. Wrongs are easily remembered, than deeds of truth and righteousness earlier offered. The character traits of some of us better fit the world, than the Church. We make more enemy than friends just because we want to have things our way, not the way Christ ordains it.

While we are at it, it is important for you to meditate on the following scriptures until you fully get it right. Harden not your heart, this is your day of salvation from this trait!

"And the fruit of righteousness is sown in peace of them that make peace." - James 3:18
"Endeavouring to keep the unity of the Spirit in the bond of peace." - Ephesians 4:3
"Let us therefore follow after the things which make for peace,..." - Romans 14:19
"If it be possible, as much as lieth in you, live peaceably with all men." - Romans 12:18

4. And Holiness

Holiness is the fourth thing God looks for. This is a big subject these days, and many do not want to talk about it, because they believe one is judgmental when correcting the carnal ones amongst us. Some want to live like the world, and enjoy its pleasures for a season.

They desire to live, the so called, full life of their dreams, without Jesus at the center. Jesus out of the equation is an invitation to crisis. Yet men advance in mad rush towards deadly allure of carnal traps, and fully ensnared by it. God is still saying, whether you want to believe it or not: *"Be ye Holy as I am Holy."* - I Peter 1:16

"...worship the Lord in the beauty of holiness." - Psalms 29:2
"Israel was holiness unto the Lord,..." - Jeremiah 2:3
"The people of thy holiness have possessed it but a little while: our adversaries have trodden down thy sanctuary." - Isaiah 63:18

Without holiness no man shall see the Lord (Hebrews 12:14) and we can also confirm it in the following scriptures:

"He that turneth away his ear from hearing the law, even his prayer shall be abomination. - Proverbs 28:9
"The sacrifice of the wicked is an abomination to the Lord: but the prayer of the upright is his delight." - Proverbs 15:8

5. Holy Spirit

The fifth thing God looks for is the indwelling presence of the Holy Spirit in your life (Rom 8:9). When you are filled by the Holy Spirit, and you walk with Him, there will be no condemnation.

"For they that are after the flesh do mind the things of the flesh; but they that are after the Spirit the things of the Spirit." - Romans 8:1

In verses 6 to 8 of the same chapter, we are informed that: *"For to be carnally minded is death; but to be spiritually minded is life and peace. Because the carnal mind is enmity against God: ...So then they that are in the flesh cannot please God."*

As long as you choose to continue in the flesh, you cannot please God. Not only that v9 of the same scripture tells us, you are not of the Lord if you walk in the flesh: *"...Now if any man have not the Spirit of Christ, he is none of his."*

6. Being Led Of The Holy Spirit

The sixth is, God wants to see whether you allow the Holy Spirit to lead you (Romans 8:14). It is those who are led by the Holy Spirit that are the sons of God. Submitting to the leading of the flesh is temporary insanity, and Paul emphasizes the fact that we are not debtors to the flesh, but the Spirit. (Romans 8:12-14)

Why are you debtors to the Spirit? The Lord sent Jesus to die for you, paid the price for your deliverance - redeemed you from sin, death, sickness and poverty. It is a big price to pay, and you cannot afford to treat this effort lightly. You have also received His Spirit and the daily load of His benefits. The Spirit you received is unique, it removes you from the bondage you used to be in. It is the Spirit of adoption, and it qualifies you as a son, whereby you can call Him Father (Romans 8:15-16).

8

CHAPTER

Ye Shall Have A New Song

"Ye shall have a song, as in the night when a holy solemnity is kept; and gladness of heart, as when one goeth with a pipe to come into the mountain of the Lord, to the mighty One of Israel. And the Lord shall cause his glorious voice to be heard, and shall shew the lighting down of his arm, with the indignation of his anger, and with the flame of a devouring fire, with scattering, and tempest, and hailstones." - Isaiah 30:29-30

The intention of God always is to give you a victory song in the time of challenges. The glory is not in singing after the victory has been wrought, but declaring His praise in the midst of your challenges. Nothing else confounds the enemies more than doing this, especially when they expected your tears.

When Praise, worship and thanksgiving precede your victory songs, it is a token of your absolute trust in Him. Praising Him while He's yet to do it, is a huge sign of your trusting Him enough to do it, and this is the key to a new song. Your reaction during this period would attract inquiries from the curious ones, who could not put together your contrary attitude to the turbulent situation you are going through. All you are openly depicting for all to see is:

"O taste and see that the LORD is good: blessed is the man that trusteth in him." - Psalms 34:8

The blessings of the man who puts his trust in the Lord are too huge for the human mind to comprehend. The world is at the feet of that man, and the stars are not by any means his limit. The commitment of these ones to God is assured, even before the battle is won. They dictate the outcome before they begin to fight at all. This is because they are aware they are fighting from the point of victory, but not for victory. They know without any doubt that Lord has already won the battle on the cross, and acknowledge His word in John 19:30 *"....It is finished..."*

Based on the above statement the believer is bold and confident to declare the outcome of a situation, even before he experiences it. If you as a believer can stick your neck out for God, declaring what His word can do for you, without batting an eye, the devil will flee from you. The kingdom of darkness will not only be scared of you, but will simply tag you as one of those who:

"... have turned the world upside down..." (Acts 17:6)

When such declarations above are made with regards to your kingdom exploits, you position yourself for divine friendship and tutoring. The Holy Spirit will instruct you at every step on what to do, and how to live a victorious Christian life. He will refine your approach and understanding of warfare. As He tutors you, and you live by His leading, His eyes will remain constantly on you, watching jealously over your life as He promised in Psalm 32:8:

"I will instruct thee and teach thee in the way which thou shalt go: I will guide thee with mine eye."

God's intention is to totally free you from bondage, and you don't have to be on a leash to be guided about like a horse. He wants you to willingly choose to follow His counsel or command, hence He invites you to receive understanding and follow His leading. He insists that you take His easy yoke upon you, and that it is better than that of the devil or the world - because the *"...tender mercies of the wicked are cruel."* - Proverbs 12:10. Therefore, the consequence of disobeying the Lord is terribly grievous. He will turn His back at your sin, while you are exposed to the result of your turning back. The verse 10 of the scripture under review better expresses the consequence:

"Many sorrows shall be to the wicked: but he that trusteth in the LORD, mercy shall compass him about."
- Psalm 32:10

The backslider in heart or the disobedient also falls into the category of the wicked, and therefore their portion is *"many sorrows."* But mercy shall surround he that puts his trust in the Lord. These are the ones that will always sing victory song. They will sing before and after their enemies are defeated.

When God fights He does not take prisoners of war. He completely decimates the enemy to his roots. The outcome of every battle that God fights on your behalf will always elicit songs of praise when you see what He has done, and the victory He has wrought for you and you will declare with joy:

"Thou art my hiding place; thou shalt preserve me from trouble; thou shalt compass me about with songs of deliverance. Selah."
(Psalm 32:7).

Songs of deliverance are thanksgiving, praise and worship. And as you thank, praise and worship Him you will be a beneficiary of His mercy, and the initiative is sincerely yours because:

"The righteous cry and the Lord heareth, and delivereth them out of all their troubles." - Psalms 34:17

"Many are the afflictions of the righteous: but the Lord delivereth him out of them all." v19

In every situation be expectant always for a new song therefore your prayer should be:

"O send down thy light and thy truth: let them lead me; let them bring me unto thy holy hill, and to thy tabernacles." - Psalms 43:3

Note that the light leads, but the truth is what empowers you, and brings you unto his prayer mountain for deliverance. The light and strength you receive, will help you to rebuke your weary soul as you patiently wait on the Lord for His signs and wonders to manifest (Psalm 40:1-3).

Through waiting patiently and praising Him - those who sow in tears reap in joy:

"They that sow in tears shall reap in joy. He that goeth forth and weepeth, bearing precious seed, shall doubtless come again with rejoicing, bringing his sheaves with him." (Psalm 126:5-6).

When you do He will do the following in your life. He will:

    i)   hear your cry and remove your feet from the horrible pit and miry clay.

    ii) set your feet on the rock and establish your goings.

    iii) finally put a new song in your mouth, - even PRAISE unto your God (Psalms 40:3).

Many shall see it and fear, and shall trust the Lord your God.

9
CHAPTER

Power Behind His Garment

"I will greatly rejoice in the Lord, my soul shall be joyful in my God; for he hath clothed me with the garments of salvation, he hath covered me with the robe of righteousness, as a bridegroom decketh himself with ornaments, and as a bride adorneth herself with her jewels." - Isaiah 61:10

Every believer is clothed by the Lord the moment we receive Him as Lord, and Savior. This garment becomes your identity and divine backing as you daily come into His presence in worship. Your access to God as a worshipper, is highly dependent on how you are spiritually clothed.

Appearing before the Lord with a stained garment is a red flag for rejection. There are several examples in the Bible where what an individual wears is called to question. The account in Zechariah Chapter 3 where Joshua, the High Priest was resisted by Satan, while he stood before the Lord because he wore a filthy garment, is profoundly relevant here. Joshua stood before the altar of God to perform his priestly duties when Satan stood at his right hand, to accuse him:

"And the LORD said unto Satan, The LORD rebuke thee, O Satan; even the LORD that hath chosen Jerusalem rebuke thee: is not this a brand plucked out of the fire? Now Joshua was clothed with filthy garments, and stood before the angel." - Zechariah 3:3

Without doubt Joshua would have rejoiced for God's intervention, and celebrated his deliverance from the attack of Satan. No one who is made free from satanic stronghold would fail to rejoice, except if he or she is an ingrate. In fact, Psalm 32:7 sounds the same note,

"...thou shalt compass me about with songs of deliverance."

Every divine intervention or deliverance by God always inspires a new song. Furthermore, the garment of the righteous is backed by power. We can in fact declare that when you put on your spiritual garment so to speak, you put on strength.

"Awake, awake; put on thy strength, O Zion; put on thy beautiful garments, O Jerusalem..." - Isaiah 52:1

When a person is dressed, it is either for battle or for peace. The one cited above is for battle. Put on your garment of power, and come out to do battle, so that henceforth the unclean and the uncircumcised do not rule over you anymore. Putting on the garment is an indication that you're on your way to battle, and are assured you would return:

"...to Zion with songs and everlasting joy upon their heads: they shall obtain joy and gladness, and sorrow and sighing shall flee away." - Isaiah 35:10

But the one who puts it on must be devoid of sin. He or she must shake himself or herself from the dust (sin), rise up and:

"...loose thyself from the bands of thy neck, O captive daughter of Zion." (Isaiah 52:2).

"You have sold yourself for nothing, but you shall be redeemed without money." (v3).

Repentance from sin is the precursor to assured victory because the evidence of sin is the beginning of spiritual paralysis. Sin cripples a strong and vibrant man, and turns him to a piece of bread. This is one reason you must flee every appearance of evil. With the garment on, and deliverance wrought, the first thing the Lord expects from you is to be a witness. It is no wonder that in verse 7 of the same chapter that God begins to describe the man on assignment for Him:

"How beautiful upon the mountains are the feet of him that bringeth good tidings, that publisheth peace;..."

It does not end there, it is a fact that putting on the garment is tied to singing God's praise. We read it earlier, and here it is again. After every victory, you would have a victory song. When power backs your garment you will sing, because victory is certain wearing it, and when victory is gotten, you will sing a new song and:

"Thy watchmen shall lift up the voice; with the voice together shall they sing:..."

"Break forth into joy, sing together, ye waste places of Jerusalem:...".- Isaiah 52:8-9 (KJV)

Furthermore, we read the same response in Isaiah 61:10 where he declares that I will rejoice in the Lord because He has: *"...clothed me with the garments of salvation, he hath covered me with the robe of righteousness..."*

What has God done? God saved him and covered his nakedness. Putting on the garments of salvation presents a message of undeniable freedom, and the certainty of God's redemptive package. These garments symbolically emphasize the four powerful packages the Lord acquired for us through His death and resurrection.

The knowledge and acquisition of these benefits make you a victorious Christian. When you operate in your Christian journey with this awareness the enemy cannot mess you up. The redemptive package is as follows - redemption from:

i) Sin/death
ii) Sickness
iii) Poverty
iv) Bondage.

These were all acquired for us by His death on the cross, and His resurrection. Having laid this foundation, we will now examine the power behind His garment, what they symbolize and their importance starting with the robe of righteousness.

1) Robe of Righteousness

What does the robe of righteousness do? It does four things to the believer. It gives the believer:

- Change of identity
- Covering of nakedness
- Empowerment and divine authority
- New responsibilities or expectations

a) Change of identity

What a man wears defines his identity. If I change my civilian garment into a military gear, my physical suddenly identity changes. Even though I may be arrested later for impersonation, while it lasted everyone who saw me would perceive me to be a military personnel. Similarly, when a person puts on a Bishop's Cassock/collar and goes into a go-go club (Pornographic Club), he would be turned back. Why? Because everyone has an otherwise expectation of a man of God. His presence there will convict others of sin, and that is bad business for the owners. Identity change is exactly what the garment of righteousness does. It presents a person with a new image, that grants him access to divine identity before the hosts of heaven. Power backs every identity you carry.

What you wear is an indication of how people will perceive you. This is the reason why some professions and organizations have dress code. If you do not fit into this expected code you may be sanctioned, and when also an unauthorized person meets the code but acts in a manner contrary to expectation he or she will have to declare his identity.

b) Covering of nakedness

Just like the cloth we wear covers our nakedness, the robe of righteousness does too. Much more, it keeps the righteous safe from the hands of the evil one, because it advertises you as a touch not! It keeps those who fear Him away from trouble, because the awareness of what they are wearing, rings loud in their consciousness.

There are many who are clothed physically, yet are spiritually naked. Their robes have been punctured by the arrows or darts of violent sins. You can easily see through them. When they get angry and display the foolishness of anger they rend their clothes the more. But if the robe is in place the kingdom of darkness can neither see through them, nor overcome them.

c) Empowerment and divine authority.

The garment grants empowerment and divine authority to war against the kingdom of darkness. Just like a government's authority backs a policeman's or soldier's uniform, God's authority backs the robe of righteousness He puts on us. For emphasis the Bible reveals to us that God commits government into the hand of those who have the robe of righteousness. *"...and I will commit thy government into his hand:..."* (Isaiah 22:21)

To continue to enjoy the flow of power as you have the covering of the robe of righteousness, you must live a holy life. You cannot continue in sin, and enjoy this power. Do you need great things to happen in your life? Watch how you run your life, and treat the robe. Sin has left dirty spots on several robes as I write, but the blood of Jesus is sufficient to make them become white as snow, if they repent.

Beyond the commitment of power and authority the Lord oversees the growth of these ones who put their trust in Him, and they gradually progress to become the friends of God. In the process of time, He makes them to become mentors or fathers to many: *"...he shall be a father to the inhabitants of Jerusalem, and to the house of Judah."*

As they watch daily in prayer, meditate on the word, fast and worship the hand of the Lord abounds in their lives. The seeds of prayer and the word sown day and night begin to bear fruits of increase, growth and receipt of inheritance among those sanctified (Acts 20:32).

d) New responsibilities or expectations

With this garments on you, God places on you great responsibilities and expectations. From that moment you cease to be an ordinary day-to-day kind of person, because a divine cloak is placed on your back with great responsibility. Your life from this point on must be sacred, and you must live in Him who has called you to service. You must therefore, be ready and willing to carry yourself with a sense of responsibility.

There is a saying **"To whom much is given, much is expected,"** which means a man with responsibility should carry himself with great discretion and understanding. He must be careful how he walks, talks and lives life in general. He is a man on assignment and he must do everything to measure up in diligence and commitment to the call. He cannot afford to be careless, and must therefore be available to respond to the demand placed on him. Everything that would make him succeed must be explored, in order not to disappoint who has called him.

2) The components of Power

What are the components of power behind the new garment? Shall we turn to Isaiah 22:20-22 to have a better perspective of the power components.

"And it shall come to pass in that day, that I will call my servant Eliakim the son of Hilkiah: And I will clothe him with thy robe, and strengthen him with thy girdle, and I will commit thy government into his hand: and he shall be a father to the inhabitants of Jerusalem, and to the house of Judah. And the key of the house of David will I lay upon his shoulder; so he shall open, and none shall shut; and he shall shut, and none shall open."

a) A Call to Service

From the scripture under review, it is clear that a divine call precedes the wearing of the garment:

"And it shall come to pass in that day, that I will call my servant Eliakim..."

Without the call there can't be the adorning of the robe of righteousness. Therefore, the first power component identified here is a call to service in righteousness. This call is the power behind the robe, and the robe is the evidence certifying the call.

When the enemies see the robe they should of a necessity flee, because they know what it signifies. It is sad to note however, that many robes are not in place as we speak, and some that are in place are stained with oil of sin or have holes punctured into it by arrows of self inflicted transgressions such as pride, anger, un-forgiveness, bitterness etc. For this robe to be effective and do what it is assigned to do, it must remain the robe of righteousness, and white as wool.

b) The Girdle.

The robe is made strong and held in place or made firm on you by the girdle (v21), and this is the second power component backing the robe of righteousness. It keeps the robe held perfectly well on you, so that the winds, and storms of life could not flow underneath it, and expose your nakedness. As we search deep in the Bible, we notice that there are two types of girdles revealed in Isaiah 11:5, and this revelation is very profound.

"And righteousness shall be the girdle of his loins, and faithfulness the girdle of his reins."

Let us briefly examine them below because they are very crucial to your success as a believer and a minister in His vineyard.

i) **Righteousness which is the girdle for the loins**, keeps you going strong in your determination to keep going on for the Lord no matter the challenges. This girdle is synonymous with *"...having your loins girt about with truth..."* (Ephesians 6:14), which is the word of God.

The loins is a place of strength, that enables great lifting sustained by your abdominal muscles. The girdle helps to hold your loins in place to do heavy lifting for the Lord in faith, so that your spiritual muscle do not collapse, and you procure hernia as a result. You can do all things through Christ who is your strength, when this girdle is in place.

ii) **Faithfulness, girdle for the reins (heart)** is a revelatory girdle that operates from a person's heart, and also reveals the content of the heart. The lack of this girdle in the heart of a believer, is revealed in the person's unfaithfulness. Where faithfulness abound no one needs to call you to attend either Church or Fellowship service. When your commitment to service in His vineyard requires continuous follow-ups or checkups then the girdle of the reins is not in place. But where the girdle is in place, faithfulness and consistent commitment to service as unto the Lord is the clear evidence.

c) The key of David

The third power component is the key of David. This key opens and no man shuts, and it shuts and no man opens. The power of this key is tied to the name of the Lord, the rock of our salvation and the builder of His Church. After Peter got the revelation of who the Lord is, without mincing words He told him in Matthew 16:18-19:

"And I say also unto thee, That thou art Peter, and upon this rock I will build my church; and the gates of hell shall not prevail against it. And I will give unto thee the keys of the kingdom of heaven: and whatsoever thou shalt bind on earth shall be bound in heaven: and whatsoever thou shalt loose on earth shall be loosed in heaven."

Can you imagine a house without keys? When the Master builds His Church He gives out the keys that guarantee access to him and to His kingdom. And what are these keys? *"Pray to the Father, in the name of Jesus, through power of the Holy Spirit."* This means the Father, the Son and the Holy Spirit are keys to answered prayer.

"And in that day ye shall ask me nothing. Verily, verily, I say unto you, Whatsoever ye shall ask the Father in my name, he will give it you." - John 16:23

So therefore, from this perspective, having the robe without the keys is powerlessness, and it will produce nothing but fruits of carnality. Mr. Flesh will hold sway in that life, but when Christ rules a life, peace rules the day. For example, when the Apostles were faced with the challenge of distributing food, they chose seven deacons to handle the service which was okay. But they committed one strategic error in the process which turned out to be very costly.

"Wherefore, brethren, look ye out among you seven men of honest report, full of the Holy Ghost, and wisdom, whom we may appoint over this business. But we will give ourselves continually to prayer, and to the ministry of the word." - Acts 6:3-4

What was the error? They committed themselves to prayer and the ministry of the word while the whole church went to sleep. There seemed to be an encouraging respite when this plan was put in place, but its downside was a time bomb waiting to explode. The initial heartwarming outcome was that:

"...the word of God increased; and the number of the disciples multiplied in Jerusalem greatly; and a great company of the priests were obedient to the faith." - Acts 6:7

So what was the outcome of this downside? The first was the death of Stephen, who the Bible makes us to know was stoned to death (Acts 7:54-60). The second was that:

"...at that time there was a great persecution against the church which was at Jerusalem; and they were all scattered abroad throughout the regions of Judaea and Samaria, except the apostles." - Acts 8:1

The whole Church scattered, except the praying Apostles. The trend of events continued as if things were normal until Herod stretched forth his hands to arrest James and Killed him (Acts 12:1-2). The ease at which he arrested James and killed him, as well as the fact that he saw that it pleased the Jews, made Herod to go ahead to arrest Peter also:

"And because he saw it pleased the Jews, he proceeded further to take Peter also. (Then were the days of unleavened bread.) And when he had apprehended him, he put him in prison, and delivered him to four quaternions of soldiers to keep him; intending after Easter to bring him forth to the people." - Acts 12:3-4

The arrest of Peter caused a rude awakening for the whole Church. The Bible reveals to us that:

"Peter therefore was kept in prison: but prayer was made without ceasing of the church unto God for him." - Acts 12:5

The sudden turnaround of events when the whole Church prayed forced the heavens open. Their prayers brought the judgment of God upon Herod, the word of God multiplied, and God gave them the gifts of men as we read in Acts 12:23-24 below:

"And the people gave a shout, saying, It is the voice of a god, and not of a man. And immediately the angel of the Lord smote him, because he gave not God the glory: and he was eaten of worms, and gave up the ghost. But the word of God grew and multiplied."

"Now there were in the church that was at Antioch certain prophets and teachers; as Barnabas, and Simeon that was called Niger, and Lucius of Cyrene, and Manaen, which had been brought up with Herod the tetrarch, and Saul. As they ministered to the Lord, and fasted, the Holy Ghost said, Separate me Barnabas and Saul for the work whereunto I have called them. And when they had fasted and prayed, and laid their hands on them, they sent them away." - Acts 13:1-3.

Furthermore, these gifts of God touched lives as they went and caused radical changes as they served and:

- they caused great joy (Acts 15:3);
- the churches were established in faith and grew daily (Acts 16:5);
- the Holy Spirit showed up (Acts 19:1-7)
- and the Word of God mightily grew and prevailed (Acts 19:18-20)

10

CHAPTER

The Triumphant Church

"Now thanks be unto God, which always causeth us to triumph in Christ, and maketh manifest the savour of his knowledge by us in every place. For we are unto God a sweet savour of Christ, in them that are saved, and in them that perish:" - 2 Cor. 2:14-15

From inception, the Lord's concept of a Church, is that of a victorious or triumphant one. He did everything needed to be done to redeem her, prepare her as a militant bride unto Himself. The work on the cross was the beginning of divine leverage for the Church at war with the devil. Even though the battle is the Lord's, we are raised and configured to fight against the wiles of the devil. Apostle Paul makes us to know, we war not against flesh and blood. There is no doubt that war against the kingdom of darkness is part of the equation. The manifesto of the Lord during His earthly walk in this respect is very profound. We read with great assurance and joy in Mathew 16:18:

"And I say also unto thee, That thou art Peter, and upon this rock I will build my church; and the gates of hell shall not prevail against it."

The Church of Christ cannot be built by anyone else but by Him. He made sound provision for His own to constantly remain in dominion. When He said upon the cross *"...It is finished..."* (John 19:30), the sentence is true in every way you wish to translate it. The knowledge and understanding of the statement, received in faith, would do so much more for a believer, who knows that all power belongs to God.

Every believer must be aware that when we fight, we do not fight for victory, but we fight from the point of victory which the Lord won for us on the cross. The aroma of victory is sweet or refreshing. No wonder we the product of the victory are **"...sweet savour of Christ..."** unto God.

May I intentionally ask, where does this sweet aroma come from? From the work of the cross Jesus did on our behalf, by choosing the foolish things of the world to confound the wise, and the weak things to confound the mighty. Through His work on the cross, Christ was made unto us wisdom and many other things of value.

"But of him are ye in Christ Jesus, who of God is made unto us wisdom, and righteousness, and sanctification and redemption." - I Corinthians 1:30

It is the wisdom of God that brought you and I forth. The same wisdom by which the heaven and the earth were made. It is also this wisdom that we receive at salvation, which fills us with the power of God, which is Christ.

"But unto them which are called, both Jews and Greeks, Christ the power of God, and the wisdom of God." - I Corinthians 1:24

In just one encounter we receive His wisdom and His power to operate here on earth as signs and wonders (Isaiah 8:18). It is your responsibility to know who you are in Christ and who Christ is to you. We know He is the power of God, and the resident advocate for as many of us who believe.

Knowing that wisdom entered your heart at salvation, what next should be your response? The need to by His grace make knowledge pleasant to your soul Proverbs 2:10.

Basic knowledge is power; but kingdom knowledge is much more - it makes you free (John 8:32). It is in the ambit of this knowledge that discretion kicks in, to preserve you from traps of foolishness, and understanding will keep you from untimely spiritual and physical deaths in the hands of the wicked -Proverbs 2:11-19.

Furthermore, what are the other things of value He did for us to secure our lives in Him? He gave us the right standing before the throne of grace against the wish of the accuser of the brethren. It is by His righteousness that you have become righteous, and by His grace you have found mercy in the presence of God. You can continue in this process trusting Him to keep you till His coming, from the ploy of Satan.

You must with due diligence: ***"...therefore come boldly unto the throne of grace, that (you)may obtain mercy, and find grace to help in time of need."*** - Hebrews 4:16

In addition, He daily sanctifies us by His word. This separates us unto Him, as we walk before Him with grace to serve in His vineyard. Without being sanctified, we become unfit for His use, and the Accuser of the Brethren will have the justification to accuse us. His redemptive work on the cross puts us in a sure footing to walk here on earth in victory.

For the above work of grace done by Him, we have no choice but to arise and seek to desperately strive to assume the position of the Triumphant Church.

What is the Triumphant Church? May I first let you know there are three types of Churches identified by Church historians. These are:

- Church Militant (Matthew 16:18)
- Church Triumphant (Revelations 12:11)
- Church Penitent (Repentant Church)

While the first two are the ones that fit the scope of this study, the Church Penitent is a coinage of the Universal Church theologians to reflect a state of repentance. This however, is a precondition or requirement for The Militant and The Triumphant Churches in order to become members. Repentance is an ongoing focus that keeps the Church in the state of righteousness if it falls out of grace.

"If we say we have no sin, we deceive ourselves, and the truth is not in us. If we confess our sins, he is faithful and just to forgive us our sins, and to cleanse us from all unrighteousness." - I John 1:8-9

The Triumphant Church is the Church that strives to triumph daily in Christ (Psalm 32:7; 42:8). To become a triumphant Church, you must know Him in the Spirit, and not in the flesh. You must be able to answer the question **'Who is Jesus to me?'** And you must allow the Holy Spirit to reveal Him to you. It is important to let you know however, that we are presently a militant church, striving to become the Triumphant Church of Revelation 12:11.

"And they overcame him by the blood of the Lamb, and by the word of their testimony; and they loved not their lives unto the death."

How do we become a Triumphant Church? We must do all we can to be:

1) **A groaning church** - a Church that prays without ceasing, and posses a vibrant corporate altar of prayer.

"Pray without ceasing. In every thing give thanks: for this is the will of God in Christ Jesus concerning you." - 1 Thess. 5:17-18

2) **A going church** - a Church that reaches out in evangelism.

"And they, continuing daily with one accord in the temple, and breaking bread from house to house, did eat their meat with gladness and singleness of heart, Praising God, and having favour with all the people. And the Lord added to the church daily such as should be saved." - Acts 2:46-47

You are expected to win souls as you grow in grace. The Church by so doing will multiply through your giving birth to spiritual children as you become either a:

    i)   telling witness - (Mark 16:15-16) or
    ii) showing witness - (Matthew 28:19-20)

i) **The Telling Witness** tells others of the salvation grace experience, and testifies about the joy he or she has found in Christ. Having come to the knowledge of God, these witnesses simply share their experiences as they live out their lives daily before many.

ii) **The Showing Witness** reveals to us by example, the work of grace that Christ has wrath in him or her. He or she lives his or her life as a witness, making sure everything he or she does is done as unto the Lord. He or she makes himself an example of the believers in word, faith, conversation (way of life, having to do with character and personality), spirit, and purity. An anonymous writer reveals what a witness of Christ ought to be as he lives under the saving grace of Christ:

"Salvation is not the position of righteousness I hold before God, but the condition of righteousness I live out daily before men."

In the light of the above, what kind of a witness are you? Watch out as you live, men are watching you as a mirror. Your careless living may turn souls away from the Lord. Be a witness and help grow the Church.

3) A growing church - when a Church evangelizes, it will grow by addition and multiplication.

"...And the Lord added to the church daily such as should be saved." (Acts 2:47)

4) A glowing Church - a Church that basks in the glory of the Lord, and shining through God's grace and power:

"And by the hands of the apostles were many signs and wonders wrought among the people; (and they were all with one accord in Solomon's porch. And of the rest durst no man join himself to them: but the people magnified them." - Acts 5:12-13

5) A giving church - a Church that touches its community both spiritually and physically.

"And all that believed were together, and had all things common; And sold their possessions and goods, and parted them to all men, as every man had need." - Acts 2:44-45

How do we achieve the five points enumerated above? It is by allowing God to work:

1. In you
2. On you
3. With you
4. For you
5. Through you
6. Amongst you

And you must be ready to pay the price in:

1. Resilient determination
2. Uncompromising devotion
3. Consistent desperation in reading, meditation on the Word, praise, worship, prayer and fasting.

As we go I want you to know that the Lord has already commanded the strength to do all the things shared in this book. Your victory has been provided or budgeted for. Therefore, all you need do is to ask Him to strengthen or perfect what He has done for you:

"Your God has commanded your strength: Strengthen, O God, what you have done for us." - Psalms 68:28

Remain blessed and highly favored.

Contact Information

To Contact Taiwo Ayeni
For speaking engagements

Please write or call

email: taayeni@rehobothbministries.org

Or

Rehoboth Bible Ministries Inc
2304 Oak Lane., 3A Suite 7,
Grand Prairie, Texas, 75051

Tel: (972) 742-7365, (972) 345-5357

Website:www.rehobothbministries.org

Bestsellers published by:
Pastor Taiwo Ayeni
(Get your copy today on-line at authorhouse.com bookstore)

Help For
Troubled Destinies

Help for troubled
Destinies begins
with examination of
what God did for us
in the beginning

Help for troubled Destinies begins with examination of what God did for us in the beginning, the foundation of empowerment laid for us to excel, where we missed it and God's follow-up rescue plan. It goes on to examine various destiny issues such as Truncated, Vandalized, Frustrated, Abused, Delayed, Stagnated Destinies etc etc.,

Specific biblical and real life references are provided for readers to identify or connect with the subject matter. Even though we were empowered to succeed from the beginning the troubles of life have hindered many from connecting with their destinies. Frustrated and dejected many have lost hope, yet there is help for you in Christ Jesus if you are willing to FIGHT.

Therefore, to achieve God's purpose for your life you must make up your mind, arise and fight in order to be fruitful and multiply, replenish the earth, subdue it and have dominion. Correct the error under the sun, take back your horse from servants, and as a prince mount on it and begin to ride to destiny (Eccl 10:5-7). The book concludes with reassuring testimonies that confirm that "God is beautiful for all situations." There is hope and help for your destiny.

SECRET OF PREVAILING IN PRAYER

It is written to encourage the believer to hold out with God in the place of prayer and prevail.

The Secret of Prevailing in Prayer Warfare is one in several series of Prayer Manuals that God had laid in my heart to write. It is written to encourage the believer to hold out with God in the place of prayer and prevail.

Victory in prayer warfare is a possibility if one can be persistent. One of the key factors in prevailing prayer is hearing God speak. Hearing him helps us to wait till our change comes. Hence, the reason the chapter on having a relationship with the Holy Spirit is included. There is a need for the saints to have a vibrant relationship with the Holy Spirit, have him guide us as we persistently engage the kingdom of darkness in prevailing warfare prayers.

DEALING WITH GENERATION WASTERS

It reveals the operations of generation wasters in men's lives and tries to explain why many people have experienced untold hardships and sufferings that are beyond human comprehension.

This work is a follow up to my two books 'Fighting Your Way to Victory – principles of victory over stubborn problems' which deals with the revival of one's prayer life, and 'Smashing the Gates of the Enemy – through Strategic Prayers' which encourages the believer to engage in strategic spiritual warfare in order to unseat the powers of darkness limiting them from entering into their inheritance.

The book is titled 'Dealing with Generation Wasters' It reveals the operations of generation wasters in men's lives and tries to explain why many people have experienced untold hardships and sufferings that are beyond human comprehension.

The 10 Dangerous Possessions

The 10 Dangerous Possessions

Taiwo Olusegun Ayeni

Going through the book will provide us with hard facts why change is necessary at this time and why we need to watch out and not fall prey to the 10 dangerous possessions.

This book unfolds the burden of reassessing how the work should be done in the Lord's vineyard. We thank God that they that sit in darkness have gotten the opportunity to see a great light. This great light has revealed to us the avalanche of recycled errors that the Church has continued to peddle with relish within the last two decades. As a result of the continuous exposure to them, they have become the norm rather than the exception.

These errors have become so entrenched that challenging them is like confronting a fast moving train headlong. Going through the book will provide us with hard facts why change is necessary at this time and why we need to watch out and not fall prey to the 10 dangerous possessions.

Fighting
Your Way To
Victory

It reveals explicitly the reality of the life of an average Christian in an urban center where stress is the hallmark of existence.

This is the first book in the series of work (Prayer School Manuals) originally titled 'The gates of Hell shall not prevail Parts I & II'. It is titled 'Fighting Your Way To Victory – principles of victory over stubborn problems' and it deals with the revival of prayer life, and the need to rise up and engage in spiritual warfare in order to overcome unnecessary sufferings.

It reveals explicitly the reality of the life of an average Christian in an urban center where stress is the hallmark of existence.

SMASHING THE GATES OF THE ENEMY

It encourages the believer to engage in strategic spiritual warfare in order to unseat the powers of darkness limiting them from entering into their inheritance.

This is the second book in the series of work (Prayer School Manuals) originally titled 'The gates of Hell shall not prevail Parts I & II'.

While the first: 'Fighting your Way to Victory' deals with the revival of prayer life, the second which is titled 'Smashing the Gates of the Enemy – through Strategic Prayers' encourages the believer to engage in strategic spiritual warfare in order to unseat the powers of darkness limiting them from entering into their inheritance.

Printed in the United States
By Bookmasters